OpenStack Networking Essentials

Build and manage networks in OpenStack
using Neutron

James Denton

BIRMINGHAM - MUMBAI

OpenStack Networking Essentials

Copyright © 2016 Packt Publishing

First published: April 2016

Production reference: 1130416

Published by Packt Publishing Ltd.
Livery Place
35 Livery Street
Birmingham B3 2PB, UK.

ISBN 978-1-78528-327-7

www.packtpub.com

Credits

Author
James Denton

Reviewer
Cody Bunch

Commissioning Editor
Kartikey Pandey

Acquisition Editor
Rreshma Raman

Content Development Editor
Mehvash Fatima

Technical Editor
Vishal Mewada

Copy Editor
Madhusudan Uchil

Project Coordinator
Shweta H Birwatkar

Proofreader
Safis Editing

Indexer
Hemangini Bari

Graphics
Kirk D'Penha

Production Coordinator
Shantanu N. Zagade

Cover Work
Shantanu N. Zagade

About the Author

James Denton has more than 15 years of experience in system administration and networking and has been deploying, operating, and maintaining OpenStack clouds since late 2012. He is a Principal Architect at Rackspace, and prior to joining the Rackspace Private Cloud team, he spent 5 years as an enterprise network security engineer. James has a bachelor's degree in business management, with a focus on computer information systems, from Texas State University in San Marcos, Texas. In his spare time, James enjoys spending time with his wife and son and camping in the Texas hill country.

www.PacktPub.com

eBooks, discount offers, and more

Did you know that Packt offers eBook versions of every book published, with PDF and ePub files available? You can upgrade to the eBook version at www.PacktPub. com and as a print book customer, you are entitled to a discount on the eBook copy. Get in touch with us at customercare@packtpub.com for more details.

At www.PacktPub.com, you can also read a collection of free technical articles, sign up for a range of free newsletters and receive exclusive discounts and offers on Packt books and eBooks.

https://www2.packtpub.com/books/subscription/packtlib

Do you need instant solutions to your IT questions? PacktLib is Packt's online digital book library. Here, you can search, access, and read Packt's entire library of books.

Why subscribe?

- Fully searchable across every book published by Packt
- Copy and paste, print, and bookmark content
- On demand and accessible via a web browser

Table of Contents

Preface   **v**

Chapter 1: OpenStack Networking Components – an Overview   **1**

  Features of OpenStack Networking   **1**

    Switching   2

    Routing   2

    Advanced networking features   3

      Load balancing   3

      Firewalling   3

      Virtual private networks   3

  The OpenStack architecture   **4**

  A reference architecture   **6**

    Implementing the network   6

      Plugins and drivers   6

      Neutron agents   7

      The DHCP agent   7

      The metadata agent   7

      The network plugin agent   8

  Summary   **9**

Chapter 2: Installing OpenStack Using RDO   **11**

  System requirements   **11**

  The initial network configuration   **12**

    Example networks   13

    Interface configuration   14

    Connect to the host   16

  Initial steps   **16**

    Permissions   16

    Install network utilities   17

    Set the hostname   17

    Install Network Time Protocol (NTP)   17

Disable NetworkManager 17
Upgrade the system 18
Install RDO using Packstack **18**
Download RDO **18**
Configure the answer file 18
Install RDO 20
Verify connectivity to OpenStack 21
Verify connectivity to the dashboard 22
Additional installation tasks **23**
Create a security group rule 23
Create a demo project and user 24
Configure the keystone_demo file 25
Upload an image to Glance 25
Summary **26**
Chapter 3: Neutron API Basics **27**
Networks **29**
Network attributes 30
Provider attributes 31
Additional attributes 32
Subnets **32**
Ports **34**
The Neutron workflow **37**
Booting an instance 37
How the logical model is implemented 37
Deleting an instance 39
Summary **39**
Chapter 4: Interfacing with Neutron **41**
Using the Horizon dashboard **42**
Managing resources within a project 42
Creating networks within a project 42
Viewing the network topology 46
Managing resources as an administrator 47
Using the Neutron client **50**
Creating and listing networks 51
Creating a network 52
Creating a subnet 53
Summary **54**
Chapter 5: Switching **55**
The basics of switching in OpenStack **55**
Using Linux bridges 56
Using Open vSwitch 56

Network types   57
Local networks   58
Flat networks   59
VLAN networks   61
VXLAN networks   63
GRE networks   65
A look at our environment   **66**
Getting a closer look   66
Summary   **70**
Chapter 6: Routing   **71**
The basics of routing in Neutron   **71**
Network namespaces   71
Connectivity through a router   72
Outbound connectivity   74
Inbound connectivity   74
Types of routers   **76**
Standalone routers   76
Highly available routers   77
Distributed virtual routers   77
Managing routers in the dashboard   **78**
Creating routers within a project   78
Viewing the network topology   79
Managing routers as an administrator   82
Managing routers with the Neutron client   **83**
Creating and listing routers   83
Creating a router   83
Adding an interface   84
Listing router interfaces   85
Examining the routers   **86**
Summary   **87**
Chapter 7: Building Networks and Routers   **89**
Using provider networks   **89**
Creating a provider network   91
Booting an instance   92
Accessing the instance   94
Using a Neutron router   **98**
External provider networks   100
Attaching the router to an external provider network   101
Booting an instance   103

Testing connectivity   105
   Observing SNAT behavior   109
Assigning a floating IP   110
   Testing connectivity via floating IP   113
Multiple routers   114
Advanced networking   115
Summary   **116**
Chapter 8: Security Group Fundamentals   **117**
Security groups in OpenStack   **118**
Using security groups   119
The default security group   121
Managing security groups   **122**
Using CIDR to control traffic   123
Applying security groups to instances and ports   124
   Working with security groups in the dashboard   125
   Caveats   128
Port security   **129**
Allowed address pairs   129
Disabling port security   130
Summary   **132**
Appendix: Configuring VirtualBox   **133**
Configuring VirtualBox networking   **133**
Configuring host-only networks   134
Creating a virtual machine   **137**
Configuring a virtual machine   **141**
Installing the CentOS operating system   **144**
Attaching the ISO to the virtual machine   145
Starting the virtual machine   147
Configuring virtual machine networking   **149**
Accessing the virtual machine   149
Configuring network interfaces   150
Accessing a virtual machine over SSH   **151**
Index   **153**

Preface

OpenStack is an open source cloud operating system designed to control pools of compute, storage, and networking resources. This powerful system fosters rapid innovation while decreasing operational and capital costs. OpenStack has exploded in popularity in recent years, thanks to its features, flexibility, and overall maturity.

In this book, we will explore the networking component of OpenStack, known as Neutron. Neutron provides an API for users to build virtual network resources such as switches, routers, load balancers, and firewalls. We will walk through the installation of OpenStack using RDO and will look at the core components of the API, made up of networks, subnets, and ports. By the end of the book, you will have harnessed the power of OpenStack and Neutron to create and access virtual network resources of your own.

What this book covers

Chapter 1, OpenStack Networking Components – an Overview, provides an introduction to OpenStack Networking features, components, and the basic physical architectures required to support an OpenStack cloud.

Chapter 2, Installing OpenStack Using RDO, provides instructions for installing the Liberty release of OpenStack using RDO on the CentOS 7.1 operating system.

Chapter 3, Neutron API Basics, looks at the core components of the Neutron API, made up of networks, subnets, and ports, and how they're used to construct virtual networks.

Chapter 4, Interfacing with Neutron, explores the use of the Horizon dashboard and the Neutron command-line client to interface with the Neutron API.

Chapter 5, Switching, looks at how Neutron constructs and implements the virtual network infrastructure to enable the flow of traffic across the cloud.

Chapter 6, Routing, discusses how Neutron implements virtual routers that provide routing between Neutron networks and the outside world using source network address translation and floating IPs.

Chapter 7, Building Networks and Routers, covers basic virtual network architectures and showcases the traffic flow from client workstations to virtual machine instances via fixed and floating IPs.

Chapter 8, Security Group Fundamentals, examines the use of Neutron security groups to secure instance traffic at the virtual switch port and walks you through creating and managing security groups and associated rules.

Appendix, Configuring VirtualBox, is meant to assist with the setup of a virtual environment using VirtualBox so that many of the examples throughout the book can be followed.

What you need for this book

For this book, the following is required:

- Operating system:
    - CentOS Linux 7.1

- Software:
    - VirtualBox 5.0 or higher
    - RDO (Liberty release)

This book assumes a beginner-to-moderate level of networking experience and experience with Linux operating systems. While this book will walk you through a basic installation of OpenStack using RDO, little time will be spent on services other than Neutron as well as any configuration of OpenStack outside of what's available via the API. It will be helpful for you have a basic understanding of OpenStack and its components prior to reading this book.

Internet connectivity is required to install OpenStack packages. An all-in-one OpenStack deployment will be performed on a single virtual machine within VirtualBox. CentOS must be installed prior to installing RDO. Alternative virtualization platforms such as VMware, or physical hardware, are optional.

Major OpenStack releases occur every 6 months, and after the N or O release, Liberty repositories may no longer be available. In the event that the OpenStack installation procedure documented in this book no longer functions properly, refer to the installation guide at `http://docs.openstack.org/` or `https://www.rdoproject.org/` for instructions on installing the latest version of OpenStack.

Who this book is for

The book is for those who are new to OpenStack and Neutron and want to learn OpenStack networking fundamentals. It introduces the reader to OpenStack networking and related concepts and technologies. Some prior networking and systems administration experience is recommended. A virtual or physical server is recommended to follow along with the concepts demonstrated in the book.

Conventions

In this book, you will find a number of text styles that distinguish between different kinds of information. Here are some examples of these styles and an explanation of their meaning.

Code words in text, database table names, folder names, filenames, file extensions, pathnames, dummy URLs, user input, and Twitter handles are shown as follows: "In a reference implementation, a Neutron DHCP agent runs on one or more infrastructure nodes and spawns a `dnsmasq` process for each network where DHCP is enabled."

A block of code is set as follows:

```
[general]

# Generic config options
CONFIG_UNSUPPORTED=n
CONFIG_DEBUG_MODE=n
CONFIG_PROVISION_DEMO=n
```

Any command-line input or output is written as follows:

```
$ sudo ifdown enp0s3; sudo ifdown enp0s9;
$ sudo ifup enp0s3; sudo ifup enp0s9;
```

New terms and **important words** are shown in bold. Words that you see on the screen, for example, in menus or dialog boxes, appear in the text like this: "In addition, controller nodes run the database and messaging servers and are often the point of management of the cloud via the **Horizon** dashboard."

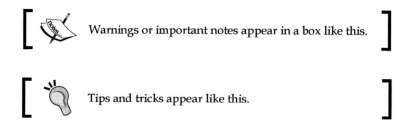

Warnings or important notes appear in a box like this.

Tips and tricks appear like this.

Reader feedback

Feedback from our readers is always welcome. Let us know what you think about this book—what you liked or disliked. Reader feedback is important for us as it helps us develop titles that you will really get the most out of.

To send us general feedback, simply e-mail feedback@packtpub.com, and mention the book's title in the subject of your message.

If there is a topic that you have expertise in and you are interested in either writing or contributing to a book, see our author guide at www.packtpub.com/authors.

Customer support

Now that you are the proud owner of a Packt book, we have a number of things to help you to get the most from your purchase.

Downloading the example code

You can download the example code files for this book from your account at http://www.packtpub.com. If you purchased this book elsewhere, you can visit http://www.packtpub.com/support and register to have the files e-mailed directly to you.

You can download the code files by following these steps:

1. Log in or register to our website using your e-mail address and password.
2. Hover the mouse pointer on the **SUPPORT** tab at the top.
3. Click on **Code Downloads & Errata**.
4. Enter the name of the book in the **Search** box.
5. Select the book for which you're looking to download the code files.
6. Choose from the drop-down menu where you purchased this book from.
7. Click on **Code Download**.

Once the file is downloaded, please make sure that you unzip or extract the folder using the latest version of:

- WinRAR / 7-Zip for Windows
- Zipeg / iZip / UnRarX for Mac
- 7-Zip / PeaZip for Linux

Downloading the color images of this book

We also provide you with a PDF file that has color images of the screenshots/diagrams used in this book. The color images will help you better understand the changes in the output. You can download this file from `https://www.packtpub.com/sites/default/files/downloads/OpenStackNetworkingEssentials_ColorImages.pdf`.

Errata

Although we have taken every care to ensure the accuracy of our content, mistakes do happen. If you find a mistake in one of our books—maybe a mistake in the text or the code—we would be grateful if you could report this to us. By doing so, you can save other readers from frustration and help us improve subsequent versions of this book. If you find any errata, please report them by visiting `http://www.packtpub.com/submit-errata`, selecting your book, clicking on the **Errata Submission Form** link, and entering the details of your errata. Once your errata are verified, your submission will be accepted and the errata will be uploaded to our website or added to any list of existing errata under the Errata section of that title.

To view the previously submitted errata, go to `https://www.packtpub.com/books/content/support` and enter the name of the book in the search field. The required information will appear under the **Errata** section.

Piracy

Piracy of copyrighted material on the Internet is an ongoing problem across all media. At Packt, we take the protection of our copyright and licenses very seriously. If you come across any illegal copies of our works in any form on the Internet, please provide us with the location address or website name immediately so that we can pursue a remedy.

Please contact us at copyright@packtpub.com with a link to the suspected pirated material.

We appreciate your help in protecting our authors and our ability to bring you valuable content.

Questions

If you have a problem with any aspect of this book, you can contact us at questions@packtpub.com, and we will do our best to address the problem.

1

OpenStack Networking Components – an Overview

OpenStack Networking, otherwise known as **Neutron**, is an API-driven system for managing virtual and physical network resources in an OpenStack cloud. The job of Neutron is simple: it is meant to provide **Networking as a Service (NaaS)** to cloud environments. Users can leverage the Neutron API to build network architectures in the cloud that define the availability of their applications. Neutron strips away from the user much of the complexity of building rich network architectures in the cloud. In this book, you will learn about some of the basic networking features offered by Neutron, and you will build a small environment that will expose you to various methods of interacting with the Neutron API to build simple network configurations.

Features of OpenStack Networking

Many cloud environments rely on virtual compute technologies made available by hypervisors such as **Kernel-based Virtual Machine (KVM)**, Xen, and Hyper-V, among many others. Neutron's core purpose is to connect virtual machine instances to a virtual network spanning the cloud and connect the virtual network to the physical network infrastructure. The containerization of applications made possible by **Linux Containers (LXC)**, Docker, and other container technologies means that Neutron should also be responsible for providing network connectivity and features to containers in the future.

Neutron relies on the use of its pluggable and extensible architecture to construct and configure virtual and physical network resources. Many physical devices, such as switches, routers, firewalls, and load balancers, are implemented in software in reference implementations. A reference implementation is one that relies on the use of plugins, drivers, and agents made available for free by the Neutron community. A common reference plugin is the **Modular Layer 2 (ML2)** plugin, which is used to define a logical networking framework that agents can use to construct the virtual network. Common reference agents include the **Open vSwitch (OVS)** and **Linux bridge** agents, which are used to construct their respective virtual switching infrastructures based on networks that users have defined with the Neutron API.

Switching

In a reference implementation, Neutron relies on virtual bridges and switches to connect virtual instances, containers, and other network resources to the network. Neutron includes support for standard Linux bridges and virtual switches created with OVS. OVS is an open source virtual switch that supports dozens of technologies and protocols, including NetFlow, **Switch port Analyzer (SPAN)**, **Remote SPAN (RSPAN)**, **Link Aggregation Control Protocol (LACP)**, and 802.1q VLAN tagging. However, much of its extended functionality and features are not exposed to users through the OpenStack API. Neutron also supports the use of overlay networking technologies such as **Generic Routing Encapsulation (GRE)** and **Virtual Extensible LAN (VXLAN)**, among others, to connect virtual bridges and switches across nodes to one another over a common network. More information on how Neutron leverages virtual switching technologies can be found in *Chapter 5, Switching*.

Routing

Neutron provides routing and network address translation capabilities that allow instances and other virtual network devices to access networks other than their own. When a user creates a virtual network, that network is isolated from all other networks. Users can create virtual routers and attach one or more virtual networks to a router. Once attached, devices in the network are capable of communicating with other attached networks and, in some cases, remote networks such as the Internet. Neutron also provides inbound connectivity through the use of floating IPs. A floating IP is a *1-to-1* relationship between the instance on the virtual network and an IP address on a real network. More information on various routing features of Neutron can be found in *Chapter 6, Routing*.

Advanced networking features

Neutron includes support for networking technologies such as load balancers, firewalls, and virtual private networks, and has software-based reference implementations for each of these technologies, using software such as HAProxy, iptables, StrongSwan, and OpenSwan. The Neutron API can be used to construct logical models that are then implemented by various plugins and agents across the cloud. The networking features discussed in this subsection will not be covered in detail in this book, but they are important features of Neutron networking.

Load balancing

Load Balancing as a Service (LBaaS) provides users with the ability to create and manage load balancers that balance traffic across multiple virtual machine instances. Users can create monitors, set connection limits, apply persistence profiles to traffic traversing a load balancer, and more. The reference plugin uses HAProxy as the software load balancer, but plugins exist that allow Neutron to interface with physical load balancers from vendors such as Citrix, F5, Radware, and others.

Firewalling

Firewall as a Service (FWaaS) provides users the ability to create and manage firewalls that filter traffic to and from virtual machine instances and other network devices. The reference plugin implements virtual firewalls inside existing Neutron routers using iptables, and third-party plugins exist that allow Neutron to interface with physical firewalls.

Virtual private networks

Virtual Private Network as a Service (VPNaaS) provides users with the ability to create site-to-site **Internet Protocol Security (IPSec)** tunnels between Neutron routers and other VPN gateways. The reference plugin implements IPSec connections inside existing Neutron routers using software such as StrongSwan or OpenSwan, and third-party plugins exist that allow Neutron to interface with physical VPN gateway devices.

The OpenStack architecture

Most OpenStack clouds are made up of physical infrastructure nodes that fit into one of the following four categories:

- **Controller nodes**: These usually run the **application programming interface (API)** services for all of the OpenStack components, including Glance, Nova, Keystone, and Neutron. In addition, controller nodes run the database and messaging servers and are often the point of management of the cloud via the **Horizon** dashboard. Most OpenStack API services can be installed on multiple controller nodes and can be load balanced to scale the OpenStack control plane.

- **Network nodes**: These usually run DHCP and metadata services and can host virtual routers when the **Neutron L3** agent is installed. In smaller environments, it is not uncommon to see controller and network node services collapsed onto the same server or set of servers. As the cloud grows in size, most network services can be broken out among other servers or installed on their own server for optimal performance.

- **Compute nodes**: These usually run a hypervisor, such as KVM, Hyper-V, or Xen, or container software, such as LXC or Docker. In some cases, a compute node may also host virtual routers, especially when **Distributed Virtual Routing (DVR)** is configured. In proof-of-concept or test environments, it is not uncommon to see controller, network, and compute node services collapsed onto the same machine. This is especially common when using DevStack, a software package designed for developing and testing OpenStack code. All-in-one installations are not recommended for production use.

- **Storage nodes**: These are usually limited to running software related to storage, such as Cinder, Ceph, or Swift. Storage nodes do not usually host any type of Neutron Networking service or agent and will not be discussed in this book.

When Neutron services are broken out among many hosts, the layout of services will often resemble the following diagram, though it can vary from environment to environment:

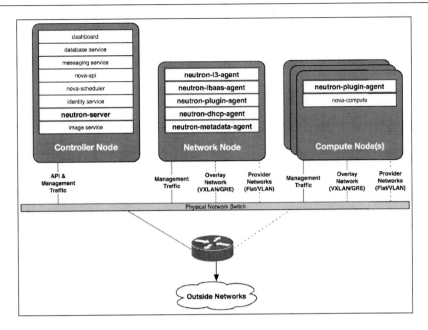

In this book, we will build a test environment on a single node that demonstrates basic OpenStack network functionality. This distribution of services will look like this:

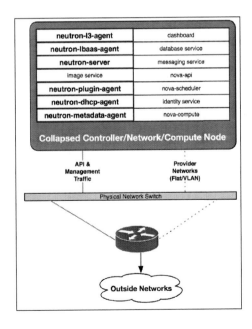

[In both of the preceding diagrams, Neutron-related services have been highlighted in bold.]

A reference architecture

In a reference implementation of Neutron, the following components can be found installed and running across the cloud infrastructure:

- One or more Neutron API servers
- A core network plug-in and driver
- One or more DHCP agents
- One or more metadata agents
- One or more network plugin agents

The Neutron API is a powerful tool responsible for taking in user-defined network topologies and passing them to network plugins for implementation. Users can interface with the Neutron API using command-line utilities, Python libraries, or directly via HTTP.

Implementing the network

Neutron supports plugins, drivers, and agents that extend network functionality and implement networks and features defined by users. In this section, we will cover these concepts.

Plugins and drivers

There are two major plugin types within the Neutron architecture:

- **Core plugins**: They are responsible for adapting the logical network described by the API into something that can be implemented by the L2 agent and **IP Address Management** (**IPAM**) system running on the host. The ML2 plugin is used in reference implementations.
- **Service plugins**: They provide additional network services, such as routing, load balancing, and firewalling, and are all available in reference implementations.

The ML2 plugin relies on different types of drivers to determine the types of networks to implement and the mechanisms used to implement them. **Type drivers** describe different types of network supported by Neutron, including flat, VLAN, VXLAN, GRE and local. **Mechanism drivers** are used to implement the described networks in software or on physical hardware.

Third-party vendors have implemented support for their respective network technologies by developing their own plugins that implement the Neutron API and extend network services. Vendors including Cisco, Arista, Brocade, Radware, F5, and VMware have created plugins that allow Neutron to interface with OpenFlow controllers, load balancers, switches, and other physical and virtual network hardware. While third-party drivers are outside the scope of this book, we will cover some of the common type and mechanism drivers in *Chapter 5, Switching*.

Neutron agents

The Neutron server is the centralized controller of the network and is responsible for providing an API to users and storing information about the network in the database. However, the actual commands to implement the network are executed on the compute and network nodes by agents that run on those nodes. Neutron agents receive messages and instructions from the Neutron server on the message bus and execute the changes accordingly.

The DHCP agent

The **Dynamic Host Configuration Protocol (DHCP)** is a protocol used for dynamically distributing network configuration parameters, such as IP addresses and routes, to network interfaces. Many cloud instances require the use of DHCP to acquire their IP address and other network information. Neutron is capable of providing DHCP services to all networks created in the cloud, and it uses a DHCP agent to manage those services. In a reference implementation, a Neutron DHCP agent runs on one or more infrastructure nodes and spawns a dnsmasq process for each network where DHCP is enabled.

The metadata agent

OpenStack provides metadata services, which enable users to retrieve information about their instances that can then be used to configure or manage the running instance. Metadata includes information such as the hostname, fixed and floating IPs, and public SSH keys. In addition to metadata, users can access user data and scripts that are provided during the launching of an instance and are executed during the boot process.

The Neutron metadata agent proxies requests from instances to the Nova metadata API, and it is accessible to instances via `http://169.254.169.254/metadata`.

The network plugin agent

The Neutron plugin agents are services that run on compute and network nodes and are responsible for configuring and implementing the virtual network on the local node. Plugin agents listen for messages from the Neutron server and construct the local network based on information in those messages. An example of how the agents work together with the Neutron server to build the virtual network can be observed in the following diagram:

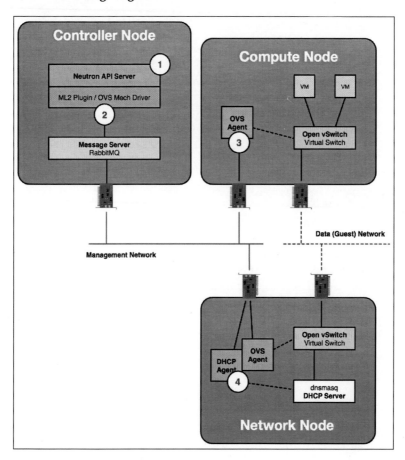

In the preceding diagram, the following actions take place among various Neutron components:

1. Neutron receives a request to connect virtual machine instances to a new network. The API server invokes the ML2 plugin to process the request.

2. The ML2 plugin passes the request to the OVS mechanism driver, which creates a message using information available in the request. The message is cast to the respective OVS agent for processing over the management network.

3. The OVS agent receives the message and configures the local virtual switch.

4. Meanwhile, the DHCP agent also receives messages related to this request and configures the DHCP server on the network node. Once this is done, the virtual machine instances will interface with the DHCP server and receive their IP address over the data network.

Summary

Neutron is one of the more complicated OpenStack components to configure and maintain, and the list of features in this chapter is by no means comprehensive. The payoff of Neutron's complexity is that users are able to programmatically build elaborate and consistent network topologies. Neutron provides reference implementations using open source components for all of the features it supports, and its extensible framework allows third parties to build plugins and drivers that can interface with other virtual and physical network devices in order to bring additional features and functionality to the cloud. To successfully deploy Neutron and harness all it has to offer, it is important to have a strong understanding of core networking concepts. In this book, we will cover some fundamental network concepts of Neutron and build a foundation for deploying instances.

In the next chapter, we will use the RDO OpenStack distribution and its included installer to configure an all-in-one deployment that will enable us to explore virtual switching and routing concepts in further detail.

2
Installing OpenStack Using RDO

In the previous chapter, we looked at the various components that make up Neutron and looked at the networking technologies that Neutron supports. Now, we will install OpenStack in a virtual machine and take a closer look at creating and managing network resources. In this chapter, we'll walk through a deployment of OpenStack called **RPM Distribution of OpenStack (RDO)** using Packstack. RDO is an OpenStack distribution packaged by the open source community for users running Linux distributions based on Red Hat, such as Fedora, CentOS, and Red Hat Enterprise Linux. RDO is a great alternative to a DevStack deployment, especially for demonstration purposes.

System requirements

OpenStack components are intended to run on standard hardware that ranges from desktop machines to enterprise-grade servers. For optimal performance, the processors of the compute nodes should support virtualization extensions, such as Intel's **VT-x** or AMD's **AMD-v** technologies. When using virtualization software such as VirtualBox, it may not be possible to extend certain virtualization features to the virtual machines running inside the OpenStack cloud, which could result in degraded performance. For demonstration purposes, however, deploying in a virtual machine can offer a similar experience to deploying on hardware, but in a simplified manner.

OpenStack currently supports numerous Linux distributions, including CentOS, Fedora, Red Hat Enterprise Linux, openSUSE, SUSE Linux Enterprise Server, and Ubuntu. This book assumes that the CentOS 7.1 Server operating system has been installed prior to the installation of OpenStack using RDO. You can download CentOS Server from `https://www.centos.org/` or from the mirrors listed on the page at `https://www.centos.org/download/mirrors/`.

A minimal ISO is all that is needed to build a fully functioning environment. At the time of writing this, the latest downloadable ISO is named `CentOS-7-x86_64-Minimal-1511.iso`.

In order to support all of the Neutron features discussed in this book, a minimum kernel version of `3.10.0-229.20.1.el7.x86_64` is recommended.

This book assumes OpenStack will be installed on a single virtual machine that meets the following minimum requirements:

Server	Virtual machine requirements	Software requirements
Single virtual machine	Processor: 64-bit x86	Operating System: CentOS 7
	Memory: 4 GB RAM	
	Disk space: 12 GB	
	Network: Three virtual 1 GBps network interface cards (NICs)	

The initial network configuration

To understand how networking within the all-in-one virtual machine node hosting OpenStack will work, refer to the following diagram:

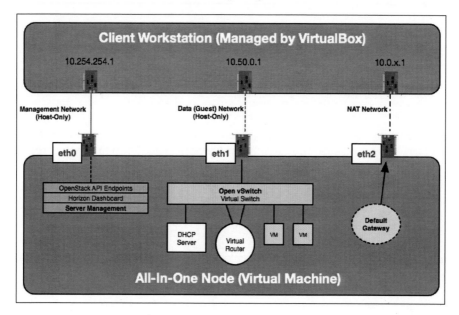

In the preceding diagram, three virtual interfaces are cabled to the **All-In-One Node**. The eth0 interface will serve as the management interface for OpenStack services and API access while eth1 will be used for interfacing with virtual machine instances over Neutron networks, including using floating IPs. The eth2 interface will serve as the gateway interface for Internet access from the **All-In-One Node** and will not be utilized by OpenStack itself. By configuring host-only networks within VirtualBox and associating them with the **All-In-One Node**, you will be able to interface with the OpenStack API, dashboard, and certain Neutron networks from your workstation.

For instructions on how to configure VirtualBox to support the aforementioned networking configuration, refer to *Appendix, Configuring VirtualBox*.

Example networks

Throughout the book, there will be examples of configuring and using various OpenStack services. The following table provides the networks used for those services:

Network	CIDR
Management	10.254.254.0/24
External/floating IP pool	10.50.0.0/24

The following tables provide IP addresses and interface configurations for the OpenStack host:

Interface	IP address	Virtual network type	Network name
eth0	10.254.254.100	Host-only	vboxnet0
eth1	None	Host-only	vboxnet1
eth2	DHCP	NAT	NA

Interface configuration

CentOS uses a configuration file for each individual network interface. These files can be found in the `/etc/sysconfig/network-scripts` directory. Interface names may vary between systems, depending on the operating system version, the underlying hardware, and the type of network interface used. Within my VirtualBox instance, the following interface mappings can be observed:

Interface	Logical	Actual
Management	eth0	enp0s3
Data	eth1	enp0s8
Gateway	eth2	enp0s9

If your interface names differ from what is listed here, make a note of the differences and configure them according to the following layout:

Interface	Actual
Management	First interface
Data	Second interface
Gateway	Third interface

Using a text editor, update the network interface files on your host as follows:

- Management interface (`ifcfg-enp0s3`):

  ```
  TYPE=Ethernet
  BOOTPROTO=none
  DEFROUTE=no
  IPV4_FAILURE_FATAL=no
  IPV6INIT=no
  NAME=enp0s3
  DEVICE=enp0s3
  ONBOOT=yes
  IPADDR=10.254.254.100
  PREFIX=24
  ```

- Gateway interface (`ifcfg-enp0s9`):

```
TYPE=Ethernet
BOOTPROTO=dhcp
DEFROUTE=yes
IPV4_FAILURE_FATAL=no
IPV6INIT=no
NAME=enp0s9
DEVICE=enp0s9
ONBOOT=yes
```

You can download the example code files for this book from your account at `http://www.packtpub.com`. If you purchased this book elsewhere, you can visit `http://www.packtpub.com/support` and register to have the files e-mailed directly to you.

You can download the code files by following these steps:

- Log in or register to our website using your e-mail address and password.
- Hover the mouse pointer on the **SUPPORT** tab at the top.
- Click on **Code Downloads & Errata**.
- Enter the name of the book in the **Search** box.
- Select the book for which you're looking to download the code files.
- Choose from the drop-down menu where you purchased this book from.
- Click on **Code Download**.

Once the file is downloaded, please make sure that you unzip or extract the folder using the latest version of:

- WinRAR / 7-Zip for Windows
- Zipeg / iZip / UnRarX for Mac
- 7-Zip / PeaZip for Linux

The `enp0s8` interface will be connected to a network bridge and used for VM traffic and will be configured automatically during the installation of OpenStack. Packstack should automatically configure the interface and connect it to the bridge, which means you do not need to configure the file beforehand.

To activate the changes, cycle the interfaces using the following `ifdown` and `ifup` commands from the virtual machine console:

```
$ sudo ifdown enp0s3; sudo ifdown enp0s9;

$ sudo ifup enp0s3; sudo ifup enp0s9;
```

Connect to the host

From your workstation, connect to the host using the management address configured on the `eth0` (`enp0s3`) interface, as shown in the following screenshot:

```
workstation:~ james.denton$ ssh jdenton@10.254.254.100
The authenticity of host '10.254.254.100 (10.254.254.100)' can't be established.
ECDSA key fingerprint is SHA256:1nbPfRKGjSZvCbpN+WT/OiyWs2r55Tn5AvAiGRO1YoE.
Are you sure you want to continue connecting (yes/no)? yes
Warning: Permanently added '10.254.254.100' (ECDSA) to the list of known hosts.
jdenton@10.254.254.100's password:
Last login: Mon Dec  7 10:38:11 2015 from 10.254.254.1
[jdenton@allinone ~]$
```

The host will utilize the DHCP interface as its default gateway interface, allowing it to access the Internet using the NAT established by VirtualBox. The management interface will be used to interact with the host using SSH as well as the OpenStack API and the **Horizon** dashboard. Once connected, proceed with installing OpenStack using the procedure outlined in the following sections.

Initial steps

Before we can install OpenStack, some work must be done to prepare the system for a successful installation.

Permissions

RPM Distribution of OpenStack, or RDO, should be installed as a user with `sudo` permissions. For tips on configuring `sudoers`, visit the following URL:

https://wiki.centos.org/TipsAndTricks/BecomingRoot

Install network utilities

Various utilities are used throughout this book to assist you in the installation and troubleshooting of OpenStack. The following command installs the necessary packages for those:

```
$ sudo yum install wget curl tcpdump
```

Set the hostname

Before installing OpenStack, use the hostnamectl command to set the hostname of the host:

```
$ sudo hostnamectl set-hostname allinone.learningneutron.com
```

Install Network Time Protocol (NTP)

A time-synchronization program such as NTP is a requirement in multinode installations, as OpenStack services depend on consistent and synchronized times between hosts. For Nova Compute, having synchronized time helps avoid problems when scheduling VM launches on compute nodes. Other services can experience similar issues when the time is not synchronized. In an All-In-One installation such as the one demonstrated here, NTP is recommended but not required.

To install NTP, issue the following command on all nodes in the environment:

```
$ sudo yum install ntp
```

Disable NetworkManager

Before installing RDO, disable NetworkManager to avoid issues during the installation and operation of OpenStack. To stop and disable NetworkManager, issue the following commands:

```
$ sudo systemctl stop NetworkManager.service
$ sudo systemctl disable NetworkManager.service
```

Upgrade the system

Before installing OpenStack, it is imperative that the kernel and other system packages be upgraded to the latest version of the installed CentOS release. Issue the following `yum` command, followed by a reboot via the `reboot` command to allow the changes to take place:

```
$ sudo yum upgrade
$ sudo reboot
```

Install RDO using Packstack

Packstack is a utility that installs OpenStack using Puppet, a module-based configuration management tool. Packstack currently supports Fedora, CentOS, Red Hat Enterprise Linux, and other Linux distributions derived from Red Hat.

Download RDO

To download RDO and other related software, issue the following commands on the All-In-One node:

```
$ sudo yum update
$ sudo yum install http://rdo.fedorapeople.org/rdo-release.rpm
```

Download and install Packstack with the following command:

```
$ sudo yum install openstack-packstack
```

Configure the answer file

Packstack relies on an answer file composed of **key-value** pairs that describe how various OpenStack and environment settings should be configured. The Packstack command has a parameter that can be passed to generate an initial answer file that can then be modified to suit your needs. You can also pass a file containing a subset of key-value pairs that can then be used during the installation process along with other defaults that Packstack specifies.

In your `home` directory, create a file named `answers.cfg` containing the following `[general]` header and subsequent key-value pairs as follows:

```
[general]

# Generic config options
CONFIG_UNSUPPORTED=n
```

```
CONFIG_DEBUG_MODE=n
CONFIG_PROVISION_DEMO=n

# Default password to be used everywhere
CONFIG_DEFAULT_PASSWORD=openstack

#Install the following services
CONFIG_MARIADB_INSTALL=y
CONFIG_GLANCE_INSTALL=y
CONFIG_NOVA_INSTALL=y
CONFIG_NEUTRON_INSTALL=y
CONFIG_HORIZON_INSTALL=y
CONFIG_CLIENT_INSTALL=y

# Configure networking
EXCLUDE_SERVERS=
CONFIG_NTP_SERVERS=
CONFIG_CONTROLLER_HOST=10.254.254.100
CONFIG_COMPUTE_HOSTS=10.254.254.100
CONFIG_NETWORK_HOSTS=10.254.254.100
CONFIG_MARIADB_HOST=10.254.254.100
CONFIG_AMQP_HOST=10.254.254.100
CONFIG_STORAGE_HOST=10.254.254.100
CONFIG_SAHARA_HOST=10.254.254.100
CONFIG_KEYSTONE_LDAP_URL=ldap://10.254.254.100
CONFIG_MONGODB_HOST=10.254.254.100
CONFIG_REDIS_MASTER_HOST=10.254.254.100

# Configure Neutron
CONFIG_NEUTRON_L3_EXT_BRIDGE=provider
CONFIG_NEUTRON_ML2_MECHANISM_DRIVERS=openvswitch
CONFIG_NEUTRON_ML2_VLAN_RANGES=
CONFIG_NEUTRON_L2_AGENT=openvswitch
CONFIG_NEUTRON_ML2_FLAT_NETWORKS=*
CONFIG_NEUTRON_OVS_BRIDGE_MAPPINGS=physnet1:br-ex
CONFIG_NEUTRON_OVS_BRIDGE_IFACES=br-ex:enp0s8

#Do not install the following services
CONFIG_CINDER_INSTALL=n
CONFIG_MANILA_INSTALL=n
CONFIG_SWIFT_INSTALL=n
CONFIG_CEILOMETER_INSTALL=n
CONFIG_HEAT_INSTALL=n
CONFIG_SAHARA_INSTALL=n
CONFIG_TROVE_INSTALL=n
CONFIG_IRONIC_INSTALL=n
CONFIG_NAGIOS_INSTALL=n
CONFIG_VMWARE_BACKEND=n
```

If your interface names differ from those listed in the earlier table, replace `enp0s8` in the `CONFIG_NEUTRON_OVS_BRIDGE_IFACES` configuration setting with the name of your second interface. The `br-ex` bridge and connected interface will be used for Neutron traffic.

Install RDO

Use the following Packstack command to install RDO using the specified answer file:

```
$ sudo packstack --answer-file=answers.cfg
```

When you run `packstack` command and pass an answer file, connectivity to the hosts specified in the answer file is verified using SSH, and multiple installation and configuration tasks are executed, as shown in the following screenshot:

```
Welcome to the Packstack setup utility

The installation log file is available at: /var/tmp/packstack/20160223-230709-NWzMCg/openstack-s

Installing:
Clean Up                                                      [ DONE ]
Discovering ip protocol version                               [ DONE ]
Setting up ssh keys                                           [ DONE ]
Preparing servers                                             [ DONE ]
Pre installing Puppet and discovering hosts' details          [ DONE ]
Adding pre install manifest entries                           [ DONE ]
Setting up CACERT                                             [ DONE ]
Adding AMQP manifest entries                                  [ DONE ]
Adding MariaDB manifest entries                               [ DONE ]
Fixing Keystone LDAP config parameters to be undef if empty   [ DONE ]
Adding Keystone manifest entries                              [ DONE ]
Adding Glance Keystone manifest entries                       [ DONE ]
Adding Glance manifest entries                                [ DONE ]
Adding Nova API manifest entries                              [ DONE ]
Adding Nova Keystone manifest entries                         [ DONE ]
Adding Nova Cert manifest entries                             [ DONE ]
Adding Nova Conductor manifest entries                        [ DONE ]
Creating ssh keys for Nova migration                          [ DONE ]
Gathering ssh host keys for Nova migration                    [ DONE ]
Adding Nova Compute manifest entries                          [ DONE ]
Adding Nova Scheduler manifest entries                        [ DONE ]
Adding Nova VNC Proxy manifest entries                        [ DONE ]
Adding OpenStack Network-related Nova manifest entries        [ DONE ]
Adding Nova Common manifest entries                           [ DONE ]
Adding Neutron VPNaaS Agent manifest entries                  [ DONE ]
Adding Neutron FWaaS Agent manifest entries                   [ DONE ]
Adding Neutron LBaaS Agent manifest entries                   [ DONE ]
Adding Neutron API manifest entries                           [ DONE ]
Adding Neutron Keystone manifest entries                      [ DONE ]
Adding Neutron L3 manifest entries                            [ DONE ]
Adding Neutron L2 Agent manifest entries                      [ DONE ]
Adding Neutron DHCP Agent manifest entries                    [ DONE ]
Adding Neutron Metering Agent manifest entries                [ DONE ]
Adding Neutron Metadata Agent manifest entries                [ DONE ]
Adding Neutron SR-IOV Switch Agent manifest entries           [ DONE ]
Checking if NetworkManager is enabled and running             [ DONE ]
Adding OpenStack Client manifest entries                      [ DONE ]
Adding Horizon manifest entries                               [ DONE ]
Adding post install manifest entries                          [ DONE ]
Copying Puppet modules and manifests                          [ DONE ]
Applying 10.254.254.100_prescript.pp
10.254.254.100_prescript.pp:                                  [ DONE ]
Applying 10.254.254.100_amqp.pp
Applying 10.254.254.100_mariadb.pp
10.254.254.100_amqp.pp:                                       [ DONE ]
10.254.254.100_mariadb.pp:                                    [ DONE ]
Applying 10.254.254.100_keystone.pp
Applying 10.254.254.100_glance.pp
10.254.254.100_keystone.pp:                                   [ DONE ]
10.254.254.100_glance.pp:                                     [ DONE ]
Applying 10.254.254.100_api_nova.pp
10.254.254.100_api_nova.pp:                                   [ DONE ]
Applying 10.254.254.100_nova.pp
10.254.254.100_nova.pp:                                       [ DONE ]
Applying 10.254.254.100_neutron.pp
10.254.254.100_neutron.pp:                                    [ DONE ]
Applying 10.254.254.100_osclient.pp
Applying 10.254.254.100_horizon.pp
10.254.254.100_osclient.pp:                                   [ DONE ]
10.254.254.100_horizon.pp:                                    [ DONE ]
Applying 10.254.254.100_postscript.pp
10.254.254.100_postscript.pp:                                 [ DONE ]
Applying Puppet manifests                                     [ DONE ]
Finalizing                                                    [ DONE ]
```

The installation should take anywhere from 10 to 20 minutes to complete and is dependent on the resources provided by the host workstation, a working Internet connection, and a working repository. If you have any issues during the installation, including messages indicating errors downloading packages or issues with the mirrors, try rerunning the installation.

If all tasks are completed successfully, a success message like this will be provided along with details on how to connect to the environment:

```
**** Installation completed successfully ******

Additional information:

* Time synchronization installation was skipped. Please note that unsynchronized time on server
instances might be problem for some OpenStack components.

* File /root/keystonerc_admin has been created on OpenStack client host 10.254.254.100. To use
the command line tools you need to source the file.

* To access the OpenStack Dashboard browse to http://10.254.254.100/dashboard .

Please, find your login credentials stored in the keystonerc_admin in your home directory.
* The installation log file is available at: /var/tmp/packstack/20160223-230709-NWzMCg/openstack-setup.log
* The generated manifests are available at: /var/tmp/packstack/20160223-230709-NWzMCg/manifests
```

Verify connectivity to OpenStack

As part of the installation, a file named keystonerc_admin is generated in the root user's home directory. The file provides environment variables containing administrative credentials and URLs for interfacing with the API. Log in or sudo as the root user to view the file:

```
[jdenton@allinone ~]$ sudo su
[root@allinone jdenton]#
[root@allinone jdenton]# cat ~/keystonerc_admin
unset OS_SERVICE_TOKEN
export OS_USERNAME=admin
export OS_PASSWORD=openstack
export OS_AUTH_URL=http://10.254.254.100:5000/v2.0
export PS1='[\u@\h \W(keystone_admin)]\$ '
export OS_TENANT_NAME=admin
export OS_REGION_NAME=RegionOne
```

Use the `source` command to load the environment variables from the file. To test authentication, issue the following commands:

```
[root@allinone jdenton]# source ~/keystonerc_admin
[root@allinone jdenton(keystone_admin)]# openstack user list
```

For the `admin` user, `keystone` should return the user list as requested:

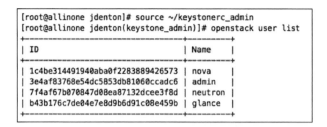

```
[root@allinone jdenton]# source ~/keystonerc_admin
[root@allinone jdenton(keystone_admin)]# openstack user list
+------------------------------------+---------+
| ID                                 | Name    |
+------------------------------------+---------+
| 1c4be314491940aba0f2283889426573   | nova    |
| 3e4af83768e54dc5853db81060ccadc6   | admin   |
| 7f4af67b070847d08ea87132dcee3f8d   | neutron |
| b43b176c7de04e7e8d9b6d91c08e459b   | glance  |
+------------------------------------+---------+
```

Verify connectivity to the dashboard

From your workstation, open the following URL in a web browser:

```
http://10.254.254.100/dashboard/
```

The following screenshot demonstrates a successful connection to the dashboard. The username and password can be found in the `keystonerc_admin` file; the password was specified in the `answers.cfg` file in the *Configure the answer file* section earlier in this chapter. In this installation, the **User Name** is `admin` and the **Password** is `openstack`:

When you have successfully logged in as the `admin` user, the dashboard landing page defaults to **System Overview**. From here, **Usage** statistics about the environment are provided in a graphical format:

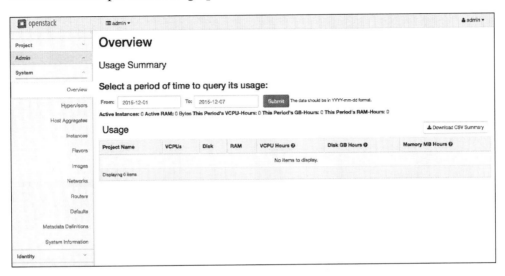

Network resources can be managed via the **Project** and **Admin** sections of the dashboard and will be discussed in further detail later in this book.

Additional installation tasks

Packstack does a lot of the heavy lifting, but before we can call the installation complete, there are some additional tasks that must be done to assist with the examples and exercises found in later chapters.

Create a security group rule

Before we can connect to the instances that will be created in later chapters, a security group rule must be added to allow that access. *Chapter 8, Security Group Fundamentals*, goes into some detail about security group usage and rule construction, but for now, we'll simply add a rule to the default security group to allow our connections to work.

Using the `neutron security-group-rule-create` command, create a security group rule in the `default` group that allows connections over the SSH protocol (TCP port 22), as shown in the following screenshot:

```
[root@allinone ~(keystone_admin)]# neutron security-group-rule-create default \
> --protocol tcp --port-range-min 22 --port-range-max 22

Created a new security_group_rule:
+------------------+--------------------------------------+
| Field            | Value                                |
+------------------+--------------------------------------+
| direction        | ingress                              |
| ethertype        | IPv4                                 |
| id               | 1dfcf2da-f4cb-4d92-88cc-d2932827b69b |
| port_range_max   | 22                                   |
| port_range_min   | 22                                   |
| protocol         | tcp                                  |
| remote_group_id  |                                      |
| remote_ip_prefix |                                      |
| security_group_id| 454fcbb8-b655-49d7-a793-9de5fd4bd837 |
| tenant_id        | 496e391ab2ee4d92afb2461811a36013     |
+------------------+--------------------------------------+
```

Create a demo project and user

Throughout the book, we will look at different behaviors between users with the `admin` role and users without it. Create a new project and user named `demo` using the following steps:

1. While authenticated as the `cloud` administrator, create a project named `demo` using the `openstack` client:

```
[root@allinone ~(keystone_admin)]# openstack project create --description "Demo Project" demo
+-------------+----------------------------------+
| Field       | Value                            |
+-------------+----------------------------------+
| description | Demo Project                     |
| enabled     | True                             |
| id          | a15a1bccb55d40dfbaf0499c2cae6fcb |
| name        | demo                             |
+-------------+----------------------------------+
```

2. Next, create a user of the same name with the password `openstack`:

```
[root@allinone ~(keystone_admin)]# openstack user create demo --password openstack
+----------+----------------------------------+
| Field    | Value                            |
+----------+----------------------------------+
| email    | None                             |
| enabled  | True                             |
| id       | f3aa8c94b4cf4a89a0b302228e459cc3 |
| name     | demo                             |
| username | demo                             |
+----------+----------------------------------+
```

3. Finally, associate the demo user with the built-in _member_ role:

```
[root@allinone ~(keystone_admin)]# openstack role add --project demo --user demo _member_
+-------+----------------------------------+
| Field | Value                            |
+-------+----------------------------------+
| id    | 9fe2ff9ee4384b1894a90878d3e92bab |
| name  | _member_                         |
+-------+----------------------------------+
```

Configure the keystone_demo file

The keystonerc_admin file created by Packstack and placed in the /root directory provides a quick and easy way to authenticate yourself as the cloud administrator in order to perform tasks using the OpenStack API. The demo user we just created will be used throughout this book to demonstrate non-administrative tasks. The following commands should be used to create a file similar to the keystonerc_admin file. It will allow us to quickly authenticate as the demo user:

1. For consistency, log in or sudo as the root user and create a file named keystone_demo in the home directory of the root user:

   [root@allinone jdenton]# vi ~/keystonerc_demo

2. Populate the file with the following content:

   ```
   unset OS_SERVICE_TOKEN
   export OS_USERNAME=demo
   export OS_PASSWORD=openstack
   export PS1='[\u@\h \W(keystone_demo)]\$ '
   export OS_AUTH_URL=http://10.254.254.100:5000/v2.0
   export OS_TENANT_NAME=demo
   export OS_IDENTITY_API_VERSION=2.0
   ```

3. Save and close the file. We will utilize it later in this book.

Upload an image to Glance

Testing network connectivity through networks and routers created in later chapters will require the use of virtual machine instances. CirrOS is a Linux distribution that was designed for use as a test image on clouds such as OpenStack and is perfectly suited for the task.

The latest CirrOS image can be found at the following URL:

```
http://download.cirros-cloud.net
```

At the time of writing this, the latest version is CirrOS 0.3.4. For consistency, log in or sudo as the root user and download the file to a temporary directory:

```
# wget http://download.cirros-cloud.net/0.3.4/cirros-0.3.4-x86_64-disk.
img -P /var/tmp
```

Source the admin credentials and upload the image with the following commands:

```
# source ~/keystone_admin
# glance image-create --name "cirros-0.3.4-x86_64" \
    --file /var/tmp/cirros-0.3.4-x86_64-disk.img \
    --disk-format qcow2 --container-format bare \
    --visibility public --progress
```

Using the Glance image-list or openstack image list commands, verify that the image is available:

```
[root@allinone ~(keystone_admin)]# openstack image list
+--------------------------------------+---------------------+
| ID                                   | Name                |
+--------------------------------------+---------------------+
| 755ab1fb-77b8-4434-93eb-062084b46b0a | cirros-0.3.4-x86_64 |
+--------------------------------------+---------------------+
```

Take a note of the reported image ID, as it will be used later in this book.

Summary

Using Packstack, a full installation of OpenStack including Keystone, Glance, Horizon, Nova, and Neutron services was successfully deployed in an All-In-One Node. Now that you've verified access to the OpenStack dashboard, let's take a look at how to interface with Neutron to create and manage network resources. In the next chapter, we will explore the network management section of the **Horizon** dashboard and interface with the Neutron API using the Neutron client.

3
Neutron API Basics

Neutron is a virtual networking service that allows users to define network connectivity and IP addressing for instances and other cloud resources using an **application programmable interface (API)**. The Neutron API is made up of core elements that define basic network architectures and extensions that extend base functionality. Neutron accomplishes this by virtue of its data model, which consists of networks, subnets, and ports. These objects help define the characteristics of the network in an easily storable format. These core elements are used to build a logical network data model using information that corresponds to layer 1 through 3 of the OSI model, shown here:

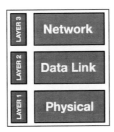

 For more information on the OSI model, check out the Wikipedia article at https://en.wikipedia.org/wiki/OSI_model.

Neutron uses plugins and drivers to identify network features and construct the virtual network infrastructure based on information stored in the database. A core plugin, such as the ML2 plugin included with Neutron, implements the core Neutron API and is responsible for adapting the logical network described by networks, ports, and subnets into something that can be implemented by the L2 agent and IP address management system running on the hosts. The extension API, provided by service plugins, allows users to manage the following resources:

- Security groups
- Quotas
- Routers
- Firewalls
- Load balancers
- Virtual private networks

Neutron's extensibility means that new features can be implemented in the form of extensions and plugins that extend the API without requiring major changes. This allows vendors to introduce features and functionality that would otherwise not be available with the base API.

The following diagram demonstrates at a high level how the Neutron API server interacts with the various plugins and agents responsible for constructing the virtual and physical network across the cloud:

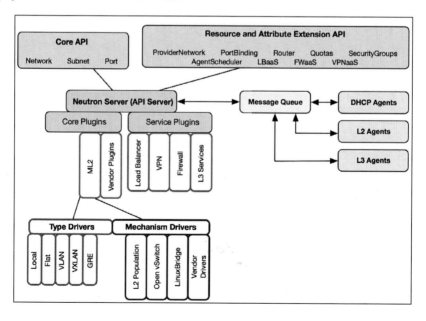

The figure demonstrates the interaction between the Neutron API service, Neutron plugins and drivers, and services such as the L2 and L3 agents. As network actions are performed by users via the API, the Neutron server publishes messages to the message queue that are consumed by agents. L2 agents build and maintain the virtual network infrastructure, while L3 agents are responsible for building and maintaining Neutron routers and associated functionality.

The Neutron API specifications can be found on the OpenStack wiki at `https://wiki.openstack.org/wiki/Neutron/APIv2-specification`. In the next few sections, we will look at some of the core elements of the API and the data models used to represent those elements.

Networks

A network is the central object of the Neutron v2.0 API data model and describes an isolated **Layer 2** segment. In a traditional infrastructure, machines are connected to switch ports that are often grouped together into **Virtual Local Area Networks (VLANs)** identified by unique IDs. Machines in the same network or VLAN can communicate with one another but cannot communicate with other networks in other VLANs without the use of a router. The following diagram demonstrates how networks are isolated from one another in a traditional infrastructure:

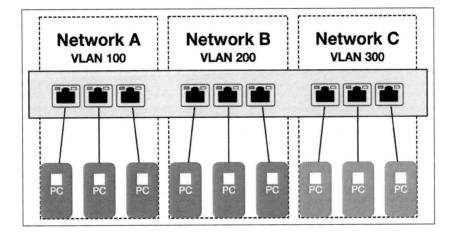

Neutron network objects have attributes that describe the network type and the physical interface used for traffic. The attributes also describe the segmentation ID used to identify traffic between other networks connected to virtual switches on the underlying host. The following diagram shows how a Neutron network describes various **Layer 1** and **Layer 2** attributes:

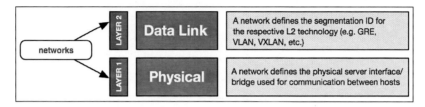

Traffic between instances on different hosts requires underlying connectivity between the hosts. This means that the hosts must reside on the same physical switching infrastructure so that VLAN-tagged traffic can pass between them. Traffic between hosts can also be encapsulated using L2-in-L3 technologies such as **GRE**, **VLAN**, or **VXLAN**. Neutron supports multiple **Layer 2** methods of segmenting traffic, including using 802.1q VLANs, VXLAN, GRE, and others, depending on the plugin and configured drivers and agents. Devices in the same network are in the same broadcast domain, even though they may reside on different hosts and attach to different virtual switches. Neutron network attributes are very important in defining how traffic between virtual machine instances should be forwarded between hosts. More information on different Layer 2 segmentation methods and how they work can be found in *Chapter 5, Switching*.

Network attributes

The following table describes base attributes associated with network objects; more details can be found at the Neutron API specifications wiki referenced earlier in this chapter:

Attribute	Type	Required	Default	Notes
id	uuid-str	N/A	Auto generated	The UUID for the network
name	string	no	None	The human-readable name of the network
admin_state_up	boolean	no	True	The administrative state of the network
status	string	N/A	null	This indicates whether the network is currently operational
subnets	list	no	Empty list	Subnets associated with the network

Attribute	Type	Required	Default	Notes
shared	boolean	no	False	This specifies whether the network can be accessed by any tenant
tenant_id	uuid-str	no	N/A	The owner of the network

Networks are typically associated with tenants or projects and are usable by any user that is a member of the same tenant or project. Networks can also be shared with all other projects or a subset of projects using Neutron's **Role Based Access Control (RBAC)** functionality.

Neutron RBAC first became available in the Liberty release of OpenStack. For more information on using the RBAC features, check out my blog at the following URL:

`https://developer.rackspace.com/blog/A-First-Look-at-RBAC-in-the-Liberty-Release-of-Neutron/`.

Provider attributes

One of the earliest extensions to the Neutron API is known as the **provider extension**. The provider network extension maps virtual networks to physical networks by adding additional network attributes that describe the network type, segmentation ID, and physical interface. The following table shows various provider attributes and their associated values:

Attribute	Type	Required	Options	Default	Notes
provider:network_type	string	yes	vlan, flat, local, vxlan, gre	Based on the configuration	
provider:segmentation_id	int	optional	Depends on network type	Based on the configuration	The segmentation ID range varies among L2 technologies
provider:physical_network	string	optional	Provider label	Based on the configuration	This specifies the physical interface used for traffic (flat or vlan only)

All networks have provider attributes. However, because provider attributes specify particular network configuration settings and mappings, only users with the admin role can specify them when creating networks. Users without the admin role can still create networks, but the Neutron server, not the user, will determine the type of network created and any corresponding interface or segmentation ID. Provider attributes will be covered in more detail in *Chapter 5, Switching*, and *Chapter 7, Building Networks and Routers*.

Additional attributes

The `external-net` extension adds an attribute to networks that is used to determine whether or not the network can be used as the external, or gateway, network for a Neutron router. When set to `true`, the network becomes eligible for use as a floating IP pool when attached to routers.

Using the `Neutron router-gateway-set` command, routers can be attached to external networks. The following table shows the external network attribute and its associated values:

Attribute	Type	Required	Default	Notes
`router:external`	Boolean	no	false	When true, the network is eligible for use as a floating IP pool when attached to a router

External networks will be covered in more detail in *Chapter 6, Routing*, and *Chapter 7, Building Networks and Routers*.

Subnets

In the Neutron data model, a subnet is an IPv4 or IPv6 address block from which IP addresses can be assigned to virtual machine instances and other network resources. Each subnet must have a subnet mask represented by a **Classless Inter-Domain Routing (CIDR)** and must be associated with a network, as seen here:

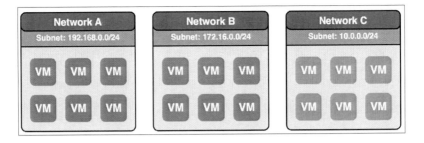

In the preceding diagram, three isolated VLAN networks each have a corresponding subnet. Instances and other devices cannot be attached to networks without an associated subnet. Instances connected to a network can communicate among one another, but they are unable to connect to other networks or subnets without the use of a router. More information on routers can be found in *Chapter 6, Routing*. The following diagram shows how a Neutron subnet describes various **Layer 3** attributes in the OSI model:

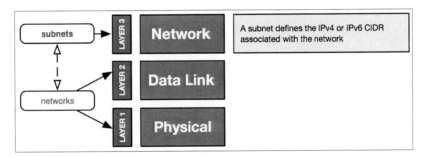

When creating subnets, users can specify IP allocation pools that limit which addresses in the subnet are available for allocation. Users can also define a custom gateway address, a list of DNS servers, and individual host routes that can be pushed to virtual machine instances using DHCP.

The following table describes attributes associated with subnet objects:

Attribute	Type	Required	Default	Notes
id	uuid-str	n/a	Auto generated	The UUID of the subnet
network_id	uuid-str	Yes	N/A	The UUID of the associated network
name	string	no	None	The human-readable name of the subnet
ip_version	int	Yes	4	IP version 4 or 6

Attribute	Type	Required	Default	Notes
cidr	string	Yes	N/A	The CIDR representing the IP address range for the subnet
gateway_ip	string or null	no	First address in CIDR	The default gateway used by devices in the subnet
dns_ nameservers	list(str)	no	None	The DNS name servers used by hosts in the subnet.
allocation_ pools	list(dict)	no	Every address in the CIDR (excluding the gateway)	Subranges of the CIDR available for dynamic allocation.
tenant_id	uuid-str	no	N/A	The owner of the subnet
enable_dhcp	Boolean	no	True	This indicates whether or not DHCP is enabled for the subnet
host_routes	list(dict)	no	N/A	Additional static routes

Ports

In the Neutron data model, a port represents a switch port on a logical switch that spans the entire cloud and contains information about connected devices. **Virtual machine interfaces (VIFs)** and other network objects such as router and DHCP server interfaces are mapped to Neutron ports. The ports define both the MAC address and the IP address to be assigned to the devices associated with them. Each port must be associated with a Neutron network.

The following diagram shows how a port describes various **Layer 2** attributes in the OSI model:

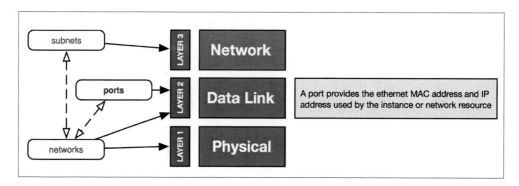

The following table describes attributes associated with port objects:

Attribute	Type	Required	Default	Notes
id	uuid-str	n/a	Auto generated	The UUID of the subnet
network_id	uuid-str	Yes	N/A	The UUID of the associated network
name	string	no	None	The human-readable name of the subnet
admin_state_up	boolean	no	True	The administrative state of the port
status	string	N/A	N/A	The current status of the port (for example, ACTIVE, BUILD, or DOWN)
mac_address	string	no	Auto generated	The MAC address of the port
fixed_ips	list(dict)	no	Auto allocated	IP address(es) associated with the port
device_id	string	no	None	The instance ID or other resource associated with the port
device_owner	string	no	None	
tenant_id	uuid-str	no	ID of tenant adding resource	The owner of the port

When Neutron is first installed, no ports exist in the database. As networks and subnets are created, ports may be created for each of the DHCP servers reflected by the logical switch model seen here:

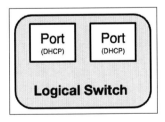

As instances are created, a single port is created for each network interface attached to the instance:

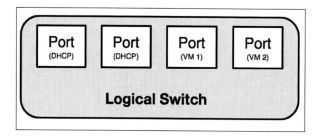

A port can only be associated with a single network. Therefore, if an instance is connected to multiple networks, it will be associated with multiple ports. As instances and other cloud resources are created, the logical switch may scale to hundreds or thousands of ports over time, as shown in the following diagram:

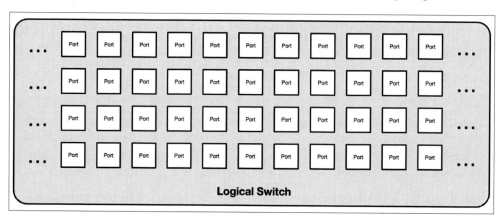

There is no limit to the number of ports that can be created in Neutron. However, quotas exist that limit the number of ports that a tenant can create. As the number of Neutron ports scale out, the performance of the Neutron API server and the implementation of networking across the cloud may degrade over time. It's a good idea to keep quotas in place to ensure a high-performing cloud, but the defaults and subsequent quota increases should be kept reasonable.

The Neutron workflow

In the standard Neutron workflow, networks must be created first, followed by subnets and then ports. The following subsections describe the workflows involved in booting and deleting instances.

Booting an instance

Before an instance can be created, it must be associated with a network that has a corresponding subnet or a precreated port that is associated with a network. The following process documents the steps involved in booting an instance and attaching it to a network:

1. The user creates a network.

2. The user creates a subnet and associates it with the network.

3. The user boots a virtual machine instance and specifies the network.

4. Nova interfaces with Neutron to create a port on the network.

5. Neutron assigns a MAC address and IP address to the newly created port using attributes defined by the subnet.

6. Nova builds the instance's `libvirt` XML file, which contains local network bridge and MAC address information, and starts the instance.

7. The instance sends a DHCP request during boot, at which point, the DHCP server responds with the IP address corresponding to the MAC address of the instance.

If multiple network interfaces are attached to an instance, each network interface will be associated with a unique Neutron port and may send out DHCP requests to retrieve their respective network information.

How the logical model is implemented

Neutron agents are services that run on network and compute nodes and are responsible for taking information described by networks, subnets, and ports and using it to implement the virtual and physical network infrastructure.

In the Neutron database, the relationship between networks, subnets, and ports can be seen in the following diagram:

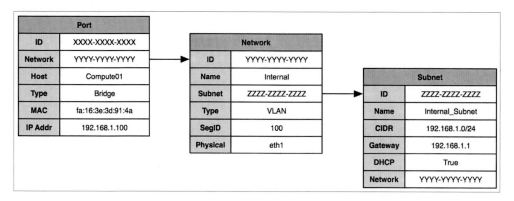

The information is then implemented on the compute node by way of virtual network interfaces, virtual switches or bridges, and IP addresses, as shown in the following diagram:

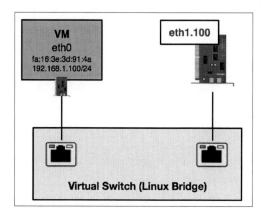

In the preceding example, the instance was connected to a network bridge on a compute node that provides connectivity from the instance to the physical network. *Chapter 5, Switching*, will go into further detail about the virtual switching infrastructure that is managed by Neutron as a result of operations executed by users. For now, it's only necessary to know how the data model is implemented as something that is usable.

Deleting an instance

The following process documents the steps involved in deleting an instance:

1. The user destroys the virtual machine instance.
2. Nova interfaces with Neutron to destroy the ports associated with the instances.
3. Nova deletes local instance data.
4. The allocated IP and MAC addresses are returned to the pool.

When instances are deleted, Neutron removes all virtual network connections from the respective compute node and removes the corresponding port information from the database.

Summary

In this chapter, we looked at the basics of the Neutron API and its data model, made up of networks, subnets, and ports. Those objects were used to describe in a logical way how the virtual network is architected and implemented across the cloud. Now that we've covered the fundamentals, let's take a look at the various ways in which users can interface with Neutron. In the next chapter, we will explore the use of the **Neutron CLI** client and **Horizon** dashboard to create and manage Neutron resources.

4

Interfacing with Neutron

In the previous chapter, we discovered the core elements of networks, subnets, and ports, which make up the Neutron API data model. In this chapter, we'll take a look at the common ways in which users can interface with Neutron to build and manage those virtual network resources.

Users can interface with Neutron to create and manage network resources in a variety of ways, including:

- The Horizon dashboard
- The Neutron client
- The Nova client
- cURL
- **Software Development Kits (SDKs)**

Depending on the operation, not all methods provide the same capabilities and access to various Neutron features. Many casual users prefer to interface with OpenStack via the **Horizon** dashboard or command-line clients, while developers may rely on SDKs related to their programming language of choice. Network resources can be managed in the dashboard in a limited fashion, while the Neutron client offers many features that are not yet, and may never be, available with Horizon. For information on using SDKs to interface with OpenStack, take a look at the official OpenStack SDK wiki at https://wiki.openstack.org/wiki/SDKs. In this chapter, we'll look at two of the most common ways of interfacing with Neutron and OpenStack in general: the **Horizon** dashboard and the **Neutron command-line** client.

Using the Horizon dashboard

Users of the Horizon dashboard can manage network resources within their own projects. If a user has the admin role, he or she can also manage resources across all projects.

Managing resources within a project

When managing network resources associated with one's own project, the **Network** menu under the **Project** section should be used, as shown here:

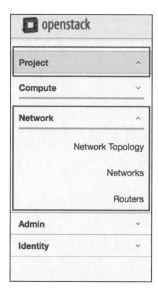

At a minimum, users should find that networks and subnets can be managed within the **Project** section, and a **Network Topology** can be dynamically generated based on the network resources managed within the project. Other resources, such as routers, firewalls, load balancers, and VPNs, can be managed within the same area when the respective services are enabled.

Creating networks within a project

Use the following steps to create a network within a project:

1. To create a **Network**, navigate to the **Networks** section of the **Horizon** dashboard under **Project | Network** and click on the **Create Network** button in the upper right-hand corner of the screen, as shown here:

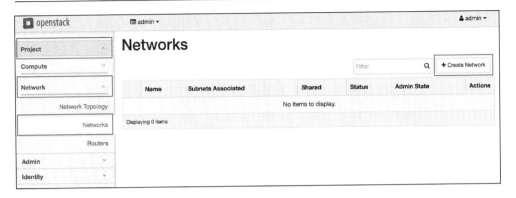

2. A multi-step network creation wizard, **Create Network**, will appear. Start by naming the network in the **Network Name** field, as shown in the following screenshot:

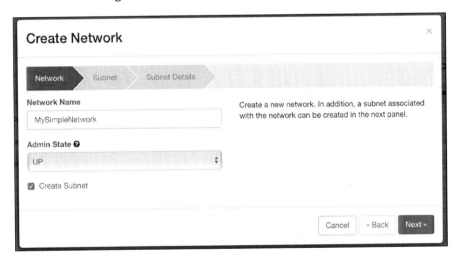

By default, the network will be marked as **UP** and will be available once it has been created.

3. With the **Create Subnet** button checked, click on the **Next** button to proceed. Next, specify a subnet in the **Network Address** field in **Classless Inter-Domain Routing (CIDR)** notation, as shown here:

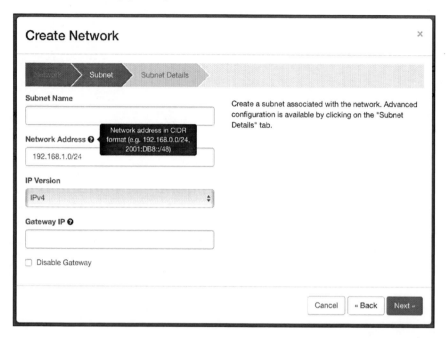

The **Subnet Name** and **Gateway IP** are optional and do not need to be specified. Neutron will automatically assign the first address in the network as the **Gateway IP**, as long as the **Disable Gateway** button remains unchecked. Click on the **Next** button to proceed.

4. Lastly, provide additional details for the subnet, including allocation pools, **DNS Name Servers**, and **Host Routes** to be pushed to instances via DHCP. The allocation pool is the range of addresses within the subnet that is available to be allocated to instances. Neutron automatically reserves the gateway address and the first and last addresses in the network as the network and broadcast addresses, respectively. In this example, we will use 8.8.8.8 for the **DNS Name Server**.

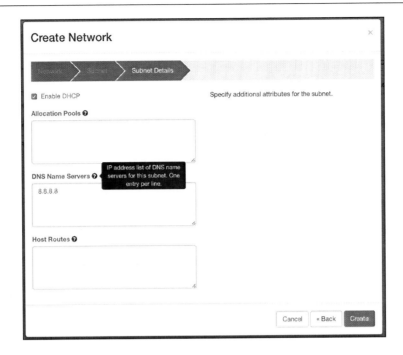

 8.8.8.8 and 8.8.4.4 are the IP addresses of public DNS servers provided by Google and are free to use.

5. Click on the **Create** button to complete the wizard and return to the **Networks** screen, as shown in the following screenshot:

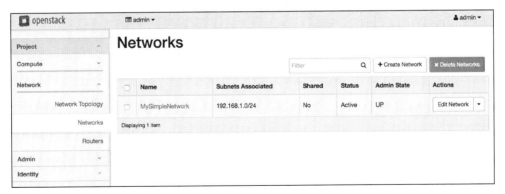

Congratulations, you just created a software-defined network! Behind the scenes, Neutron has chosen a Layer 2 networking technology, assigned a unique segmentation ID, and created a DHCP server that is ready to hand out addresses to instances placed in the network. Luckily for us, it did this without any manual intervention on the part of the user or the administrator. In *Chapter 5, Switching,* we'll take a closer look at the common Layer 2 networking technologies supported by Neutron, the virtual switching infrastructure, and why this dynamic behavior is useful. For now, relish your accomplishment!

Viewing the network topology

Now that we have created a network, let's view the resulting **Network Topology**. From the **Project | Network** menu, choose **Network Topology**. The result is a single network object, shown in the following screenshot:

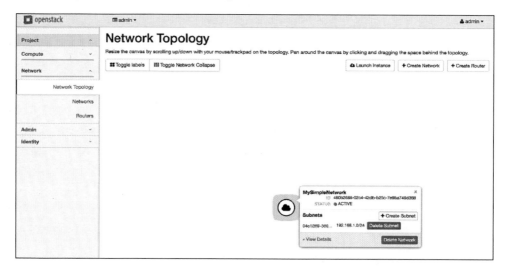

Considering our limited use of the environment so far, the topology is pretty simple and consists of a single network object. From the **Network Topology** screen, additional networks and routers can be created, which will in turn increase the complexity of the network and resulting diagram.

For now, let's learn more about interfacing with Neutron and save more complex network topologies for later chapters.

 Generating a network topology is a unique feature of Horizon and is not available from the Neutron CLI.

Managing resources as an administrator

Users with the admin role have additional capabilities and are exposed to an **Admin** panel within the **Horizon** dashboard:

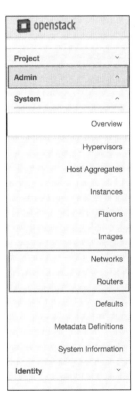

Within the **Admin** panel, administrators can view and manage not only certain Neutron resources such as **Networks** and **Routers**, but other OpenStack resources such as host aggregates, instances, flavors, and images.

From the **Networks** window under **Admin | System**, administrators can view all the networks in the cloud as well as create and delete selected networks, as shown here:

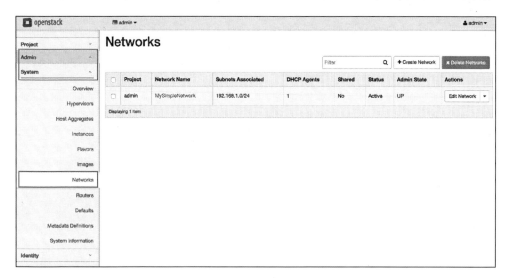

Here, we can see the previously created network, **MySimpleNetwork**. Clicking on the network name reveals details about the network not available to ordinary users, including provider attributes, related ports, and associated agents:

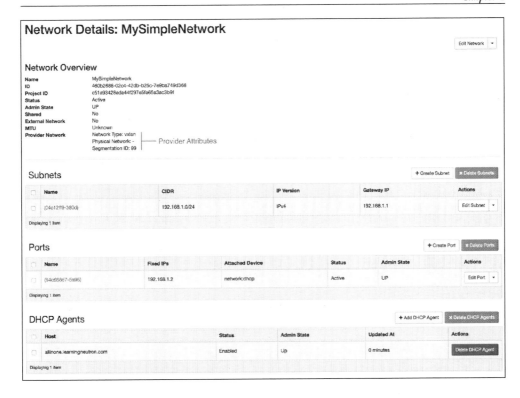

Network Details: MySimpleNetwork

Edit Network ▾

Network Overview

Name	MySimpleNetwork
ID	460b2688-02o4-42db-b25c-7e9ba749d368
Project ID	c51a93428ada44f297e5fe65a3ac3b9f
Status	Active
Admin State	UP
Shared	No
External Network	No
MTU	Unknown
Provider Network	Network Type: vxlan
	Physical Network: - ——— Provider Attributes
	Segmentation ID: 99

Subnets

+ Create Subnet   ✖ Delete Subnets

	Name	CIDR	IP Version	Gateway IP	Actions
☐	(04c12ff9-380d)	192.168.1.0/24	IPv4	192.168.1.1	Edit Subnet ▾

Displaying 1 item

Ports

+ Create Port   ✖ Delete Ports

	Name	Fixed IPs	Attached Device	Status	Admin State	Actions
☐	(94c968d7-6a95)	192.168.1.2	network:dhcp	Active	UP	Edit Port ▾

Displaying 1 item

DHCP Agents

+ Add DHCP Agent   ✖ Delete DHCP Agents

	Host	Status	Admin State	Updated At	Actions
☐	allinone.learningneutron.com	Enabled	Up	0 minutes	Delete DHCP Agent

Displaying 1 item

From the **Network Details** window, administrators can create additional subnets and ports as well as associate the network with multiple DHCP agents, when available, for DHCP service redundancy. Various resources can be deleted, but only when other resources that depend on them have been deleted first. This means that before a network or subnet is deleted, any instance attached to the network must be detached or deleted first. In addition, any router attached to a subnet must be detached before the subnet or network can be deleted. Certain ports cannot be deleted manually, especially when associated with routers or DHCP servers. These checks are in place to ensure data consistency, and they require users to follow particular workflows when creating or deleting network objects.

While the **Horizon** dashboard allows users to manage high-level network resources such as networks, subnets, and routers, it lacks some of the advanced functionality of the Neutron client. In the next few sections, we will take a look at the Neutron client in further detail.

Using the Neutron client

Neutron provides a command-line client for interfacing with its API. It is typically installed as part of the OpenStack distribution.

> The Neutron client can also be installed on your local workstation, provided you have a supported operating system. For more information on installing the client locally, refer to the OpenStack documentation at http://docs.openstack.org/user-guide/common/cli_install_openstack_command_line_clients.html.

When authenticated, Neutron commands can be run directly from the Linux command line, or the Neutron shell can be invoked by issuing the neutron command, like this:

```
[root@allinone ~(keystone_admin)]# neutron
(neutron)
```

The neutron shell provides commands that can be used to create, read, update, and delete the networking configuration within the OpenStack cloud. By typing ? or help within the Neutron shell, a list of commands available within the client can be found, as shown here:

```
[root@allinone ~(keystone_admin)]# neutron
(neutron) ?

Shell commands (type help <topic>):
========================================
cmdenvironment  edit  hi       l     list  pause  r    save  shell     show
ed              help  history  li    load  py     run  set   shortcuts

Undocumented commands:
======================
EOF  eof  exit  q  quit

Application commands (type help <topic>):
=========================================
address-scope-create          floatingip-associate        lbaas-agent-hosting-loadbalancer  nuage-netpartition-create   security-group-create
address-scope-delete          floatingip-create           lbaas-healthmonitor-create        nuage-netpartition-delete   security-group-delete
address-scope-list            floatingip-delete           lbaas-healthmonitor-delete        nuage-netpartition-list     security-group-list
address-scope-show            floatingip-disassociate     lbaas-healthmonitor-list          nuage-netpartition-show     security-group-rule-create
address-scope-update          floatingip-list             lbaas-healthmonitor-show          port-create                 security-group-rule-delete
agent-delete                  floatingip-show             lbaas-healthmonitor-update        port-delete                 security-group-rule-list
agent-list                    gateway-device-create       lbaas-listener-create             port-list                   security-group-rule-show
agent-show                    gateway-device-delete       lbaas-listener-delete             port-show                   security-group-update
agent-update                  gateway-device-list         lbaas-listener-list               port-update                 service-provider-list
bash-completion               gateway-device-show         lbaas-listener-show               qos-available-rule-types    subnet-create
cisco-credential-create       gateway-device-update       lbaas-listener-update             qos-bandwidth-limit-rule-create  subnet-delete
cisco-credential-delete       help                        lbaas-loadbalancer-create         qos-bandwidth-limit-rule-delete  subnet-list
cisco-credential-list         ipsec-site-connection-create lbaas-loadbalancer-delete        qos-bandwidth-limit-rule-list    subnet-show
cisco-credential-show         ipsec-site-connection-delete lbaas-loadbalancer-list          qos-bandwidth-limit-rule-show    subnet-update
cisco-network-profile-create  ipsec-site-connection-list  lbaas-loadbalancer-list-on-agent  qos-bandwidth-limit-rule-update  subnetpool-create
cisco-network-profile-delete  ipsec-site-connection-show  lbaas-loadbalancer-show           qos-policy-create           subnetpool-delete
cisco-network-profile-list    ipsec-site-connection-update lbaas-loadbalancer-update        qos-policy-delete           subnetpool-list
cisco-network-profile-show    l3-agent-list-hosting-router lbaas-member-create              qos-policy-list             subnetpool-show
cisco-network-profile-update  l3-agent-router-add         lbaas-member-delete               qos-policy-show             subnetpool-update
cisco-policy-profile-list     l3-agent-router-remove      lbaas-member-list                 qos-policy-update           vpn-ikepolicy-create
cisco-policy-profile-show     lb-agent-hosting-pool       lbaas-member-show                 queue-create                vpn-ikepolicy-delete
cisco-policy-profile-update   lb-healthmonitor-associate  lbaas-member-update               queue-delete                vpn-ikepolicy-list
dhcp-agent-list-hosting-net   lb-healthmonitor-create     lbaas-pool-create                 queue-list                  vpn-ikepolicy-show
dhcp-agent-network-add        lb-healthmonitor-delete     lbaas-pool-delete                 quota-delete                vpn-ikepolicy-update
dhcp-agent-network-remove     lb-healthmonitor-disassociate lbaas-pool-list                 quota-list                  vpn-ipsecpolicy-create
ext-list                      lb-healthmonitor-list       lbaas-pool-show                    quota-show                  vpn-ipsecpolicy-delete
ext-show                      lb-healthmonitor-show       lbaas-pool-update                  quota-update                vpn-ipsecpolicy-list
firewall-create               lb-healthmonitor-update     meter-label-create                rbac-create                 vpn-ipsecpolicy-show
firewall-delete               lb-member-create            meter-label-delete                rbac-delete                 vpn-ipsecpolicy-update
firewall-policy-create        lb-member-delete            meter-label-list                  rbac-list                   vpn-service-create
firewall-policy-delete        lb-member-list              meter-label-rule-create          rbac-show                   vpn-service-delete
firewall-policy-insert-rule   lb-member-show              meter-label-rule-delete          rbac-update                 vpn-service-list
firewall-policy-list          lb-member-update            meter-label-rule-list            router-create               vpn-service-show
firewall-policy-remove-rule   lb-pool-create              meter-label-rule-show            router-delete               vpn-service-update
firewall-policy-show          lb-pool-delete              meter-label-show                 router-gateway-clear
firewall-policy-update        lb-pool-list                net-create                       router-gateway-set
firewall-rule-create          lb-pool-list-on-agent       net-delete                       router-interface-add
firewall-rule-delete          lb-pool-show                net-external-list                router-interface-delete
firewall-rule-list            lb-pool-stats               net-gateway-connect              router-list
firewall-rule-show            lb-vip-create               net-gateway-create               router-list-on-l3-agent
firewall-rule-update          lb-vip-delete               net-gateway-delete               router-port-list
firewall-show                 lb-vip-list                 net-gateway-disconnect           router-show
firewall-update               lb-vip-show                 net-gateway-list                 router-update
                              lb-vip-update               net-gateway-show
                                                          net-gateway-update
                                                          net-list
                                                          net-list-on-dhcp-agent
                                                          net-show
                                                          net-update
```

Running the `neutron help` command from the Linux command line provides a brief description of each command's function. The returned list of commands does not imply that the respective features are available, however. Some commands require third-party plugins to be installed, such as the commands related to `cisco` and `nuage`. Other commands, such as the `load balancer` and VPN commands, require their respective drivers and service plugins to be installed and configured. Attempting to use commands related to features that have not been configured or installed may result in an HTTP `404` error:

```
(neutron) lb-pool-list
404 Not Found
The resource could not be found

(neutron) vpn-ikepolicy-list
404 Not Found
The resource could not be found.
```

All users of the Neutron client have access to the same commands, but depending on the user and their role, the Neutron API server may limit or restrict their use. Examples of this would include the inability of users to specify provider attributes when creating networks, specify other tenant IDs when creating objects, and more.

Creating and listing networks

Listing networks with the Neutron client is as easy as using the Neutron `net-list` command, as shown here:

```
[root@allinone ~(keystone_admin)]# neutron net-list
+--------------------------------------+---------------+------------------------------------------------------+
| id                                   | name          | subnets                                              |
+--------------------------------------+---------------+------------------------------------------------------+
| 460b2688-02c4-42db-b25c-7e9ba749d368 | MySimpleNetwork | 04c12ff9-380d-4a4e-a8aa-f31536406ad4 192.168.1.0/24 |
+--------------------------------------+---------------+------------------------------------------------------+
```

Running the `net-list` command as an administrator will return all networks known to Neutron, while running the command as an ordinary user will only return networks associated with the user's tenant or project. As an example, let's authenticate as the demo user and run the same command to see what is returned:

```
[root@allinone ~(keystone_admin)]# source keystonerc_demo
[root@allinone ~(keystone_demo)]# neutron net-list

[root@allinone ~(keystone_demo)]#
```

As expected, no networks were returned. Networks, like other OpenStack resources, are associated with a single tenant or project and can only be viewed or managed by the respective users of those projects. In some cases, networks can be shared with one or more projects, but that functionality won't be discussed here. What's important to know is that in most cases, ordinary users are restricted to only seeing and managing network objects directly associated with their respective projects.

Creating a network

Creating a network with the Neutron client can be accomplished with the Neutron `net-create` command. In this example, the demo user is logged in and the network to be created is named `MyDemoNetwork`:

```
[root@allinone ~(keystone_demo)]# neutron net-create MyDemoNetwork
```

The operation returns a response that can be seen in the following output:

```
Created a new network:
+-----------------+--------------------------------------+
| Field           | Value                                |
+-----------------+--------------------------------------+
| admin_state_up  | True                                 |
| id              | c8cde907-9a30-4e86-8c31-11d11f56cb2c |
| mtu             | 0                                    |
| name            | MyDemoNetwork                        |
| router:external | False                                |
| shared          | False                                |
| status          | ACTIVE                               |
| subnets         |                                      |
| tenant_id       | b8e0562dab644c87aa693abf48d3040d     |
+-----------------+--------------------------------------+
```

Notice that the output did not return information regarding the network type, segmentation ID, or physical interface. As an ordinary user, that information is not exposed by Neutron and is only available to users with the admin role.

> In most cases, users should not be concerned with network provider attributes and should simply require connectivity between instances across hypervisors without caring what the underlying technology is, be it VLAN, VXLAN, or something else. In some cases, revealing that information can even be seen as a security risk. Just like Nova does not reveal hypervisor information to users, Neutron does not, and should not, reveal certain network information.

Copy the `id` and `name` values from the output. You will use the network ID when you create a subnet, provision a virtual machine instance, or perform certain other network activities. In some cases, the network name can be used in lieu of the ID, but only when the name is unique. In this example, the ID is `c8cde907-9a30-4e86-8c31-11d11f56cb2c`, but the value will be unique in your response.

Creating a subnet

Creating a subnet with the Neutron client can be accomplished with the Neutron `subnet-create` command. To create a subnet, you must specify a CIDR and associated network ID or name. Other attributes are optional, including the subnet name, IP allocation pools, and gateway IP.

In this example, the CIDR is `192.168.8.0/24`, the associated network name is `MyDemoNetwork`, and the subnet name is `MyDemoSubnet`:

```
[root@allinone ~(keystone_demo)]# neutron subnet-create MyDemoNetwork
192.168.8.0/24 --name MyDemoSubnet
```

The operation returns a response that can be seen in the following output:

```
Created a new subnet:
+-------------------+--------------------------------------------------+
| Field             | Value                                            |
+-------------------+--------------------------------------------------+
| allocation_pools  | {"start": "192.168.8.2", "end": "192.168.8.254"} |
| cidr              | 192.168.8.0/24                                   |
| dns_nameservers   |                                                  |
| enable_dhcp       | True                                             |
| gateway_ip        | 192.168.8.1                                      |
| host_routes       |                                                  |
| id                | 6ee10d34-4d82-4901-9627-22a758096e52             |
| ip_version        | 4                                                |
| ipv6_address_mode |                                                  |
| ipv6_ra_mode      |                                                  |
| name              | MyDemoSubnet                                     |
| network_id        | c8cde907-9a30-4e86-8c31-11d11f56cb2c             |
| subnetpool_id     |                                                  |
| tenant_id         | b8e0562dab644c87aa693abf48d3040d                 |
+-------------------+--------------------------------------------------+
```

You will use the subnet ID when you attach a router to the subnet or, in some cases, manually create a port. In this example, the ID is `6ee10d34-4d82-4901-9627-22a758096e52`, but the value will be unique in your response.

To list subnets, use the Neutron `subnet-list` command:

```
[root@allinone ~(keystone_demo)]# neutron subnet-list
```

The operation returns a response that can be seen in the following output:

```
+--------------------------------------+--------------+----------------+---------------------------------------------+
| id                                   | name         | cidr           | allocation_pools                            |
+--------------------------------------+--------------+----------------+---------------------------------------------+
| 6ee10d34-4d82-4901-9627-22a758096e52 | MyDemoSubnet | 192.168.8.0/24 | {"start": "192.168.8.2", "end": "192.168.8.254"} |
+--------------------------------------+--------------+----------------+---------------------------------------------+
```

Additional details of the subnet can be revealed using the Neutron `subnet-show` command with the ID or unique name, as shown here:

```
[root@allinone ~(keystone_demo)]# neutron subnet-show MyDemoSubnet
+-------------------+---------------------------------------------------+
| Field             | Value                                             |
+-------------------+---------------------------------------------------+
| allocation_pools  | {"start": "192.168.8.2", "end": "192.168.8.254"}  |
| cidr              | 192.168.8.0/24                                    |
| dns_nameservers   |                                                   |
| enable_dhcp       | True                                              |
| gateway_ip        | 192.168.8.1                                       |
| host_routes       |                                                   |
| id                | 6ee10d34-4d82-4901-9627-22a758096e52              |
| ip_version        | 4                                                 |
| ipv6_address_mode |                                                   |
| ipv6_ra_mode      |                                                   |
| name              | MyDemoSubnet                                      |
| network_id        | c8cde907-9a30-4e86-8c31-11d11f56cb2c              |
| subnetpool_id     |                                                   |
| tenant_id         | b8e0562dab644c87aa693abf48d3040d                  |
+-------------------+---------------------------------------------------+
```

By default, users can see subnets associated with their tenant or project as well as subnets associated with networks that are shared. Users with the admin role can see all subnets known to Neutron.

Summary

In this chapter, we looked at the two most common ways of interfacing with Neutron: the Horizon dashboard and the Neutron command-line client. The Horizon dashboard offers a straightforward method of managing project-level network objects such as networks, subnets, and routers. The command-line client is recommended, and sometimes required, to access and manage advanced networking features or other functionality not yet available in the dashboard.

In the next chapter, we will take a closer look at how Neutron implements networks and the virtual switching infrastructure. The focus will be on the use of Open vSwitch since it is installed by default with RDO, but we will also look at an alternative to OVS known as **Linux bridge** to see how they compare with one another for simple network configurations. In subsequent chapters, we will revisit the dashboard and command-line client when managing routers, floating IPs, and other resources that we have yet to discuss.

5
Switching

In the previous chapter, we learned that users can interact with Neutron in a variety of ways to build virtual networks that connect virtual machine instances to one another and to the network at large. In this chapter, we'll take a closer look at how Neutron implements the virtual network infrastructure to enable the flow of traffic across the cloud.

When users create and connect virtual machine instances to networks, Neutron automatically creates and configures virtual switches on the physical infrastructure nodes. Ordinary users of OpenStack are not exposed to any of the underlying infrastructure, be it physical or virtual, and must rely on the *magic* of Neutron to ensure traffic gets to where it needs to go. Operators, on the other hand, may have access to the infrastructure and may be asked to troubleshoot issues from time to time. Understanding how Neutron plumbs everything together is a fundamental requirement for operating and supporting OpenStack clouds.

The basics of switching in OpenStack

In the context of computer networking, a switch is defined as a device that connects multiple devices together and uses packet switching techniques to receive, process, and forward data from one device to another. Traditionally, switches have been physical in nature and range in size from that of a physical network rack or larger to the switch built into our home routers, or even smaller. In a reference implementation, Neutron relies on the use of virtual switches to forward packets to virtual machine instances and other virtualized devices hosted on infrastructure nodes. Those nodes, in turn, are connected to physical switches that forward traffic between nodes and other physical devices such as routers and firewalls. How Neutron configures these virtual switches depends on the virtual switching platform in use within the environment and the type of network requested by the user. In the following sections, we'll take a look at the two most popular virtual switching platforms: **Open vSwitch** and **LinuxBridge**.

Using Linux bridges

A bridge in Linux is analogous to a virtual switch, and the terms are used interchangeably throughout this book and other OpenStack documentation. It has ports, a **Forwarding Database (FDB)** table that is akin to a **CAM** or **MAC** address table, and operates at Layer 2 of the OSI model. Network segmentation with the **LinuxBridge** driver is handled by the creation of a single virtual switch per network on every host.

When Neutron is configured to utilize the **Modular Layer 2 (ML2)** plugin and LinuxBridge driver, a service known as the **LinuxBridge agent** runs on each host and is responsible for using the 8021q, and vxlan kernel modules and the brctl and bridge commands to create and connect virtual switches to instances and the physical network.

Using Open vSwitch

Open vSwitch, also known as OVS, is an open source multilayer switch. Much like a physical switch, a virtual switch implemented with Open vSwitch utilizes the concepts of switch ports, uplinks, cross-connects, and more. These virtual switches support technologies such as 802.1q, SPAN, RSPAN, sFlow, and more, but not all features are supported or leveraged by Neutron.

Open vSwitch virtual switches can operate in two modes: **normal mode** and **flow mode**. In normal mode, an OVS virtual switch acts like a regular Layer 2 learning switch. As frames are forwarded through the virtual switch, the switch builds a table of source MAC address and port relationships for future lookups. If a destination MAC address is not in the table, the switch floods the traffic out of all ports until it discovers the correct port.

In flow mode, a flow table is used that consists of a set of rules or actions to perform on a packet. Actions typically result in packet manipulation of some kind, such as stripping or modifying existing VLAN tags or forwarding the traffic to a particular port. Neutron, as a source of truth for the state of networking in the cloud, is responsible for programming flow rules on virtual switches since it knows which virtual machine instances exist on particular nodes and is aware of all virtual networks and physical network mappings. A lot of the magic of advanced Neutron services is handled by manipulating packets using flow rules on OVS virtual switches. The use of software to program forwarding logic and manipulate traffic is a key element of the idea of **Software-Defined Networking (SDN)**.

With OVS, Neutron implements one or more virtual switches on each host, depending on the type of networks used. In most cases, a single virtual switch, called the integration bridge, is used to connect virtual machine instances to the network. Network segmentation is handled by the creation of a unique local VLAN, per network, on every host. The integration bridge is then cross-connected to one or more virtual switches, known as **provider bridges**. A **provider bridge** is connected to a single physical interface and provides connectivity to the physical network. The cross-connect between switches means that traffic can flow from an instance to the physical network, and vice versa, through both sets of switches. Neutron creates and maintains flow rules that dictate how and where traffic is forwarded; whether the traffic should be tagged, untagged, or dropped; and more.

When the network is configured to utilize the ML2 plugin and Open vSwitch driver, a service known as the Open vSwitch agent runs on each host. The agent is responsible for using the `openvswitch` kernel modules along with `userspace` utilities such as `ovs-vsctl` and `ovs-ofctl` to properly manage the Open vSwitch database and flow tables and to connect instances and other network resources to virtual switches and the physical network.

Network types

Neutron network types are used to define the technology used to segment traffic between networks and describe, at a glance, how virtual switches are connected between hosts. Neutron supports a variety of network types, including:

- Local
- Flat
- VLAN
- VXLAN
- GRE

Remember, ordinary users often do not have the ability to specify the type of network they are creating. In fact, users are not expected to know anything about the infrastructure other than what is represented by the API. Instead, the administrator is responsible for choosing a default type of network based on physical limitations and/or virtual network requirements. On the other hand, users with the admin role are able to create any type of network, whether or not it is a good idea and is actually supportable by the underlying infrastructure. As you read the following network type descriptions, keep in mind their strengths and weaknesses as you look to build or administrate your own cloud in the future.

As we talk about these network types and the architectural differences between Open vSwitch and LinuxBridge deployments, keep your hands off the keyboard! There is nothing to do in your test environment just yet.

Local networks

A **local network** is a network that Neutron does not connect to the physical network in any way. By its very nature, it is the simplest type of network to implement. On a host using the `LinuxBridge` driver, Neutron implements a virtual switch for each local network. Devices connected to the local network can communicate with one another but not with any other network:

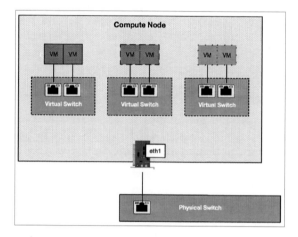

In the preceding diagram, the virtual switches are not connected to the physical interface. As a result, traffic from the virtual machine instances is limited to their respective virtual switches.

The use of dedicated virtual switches per network differs greatly from an Open vSwitch implementation. With Open vSwitch, there is a single virtual switch for all instances on a host. Each local network corresponds to a local VLAN on every node. Neutron does not create any flow rules for local networks. This means that traffic between instances in the same local network, or local VLAN, can communicate with one another but not with anything else across the virtual or physical network:

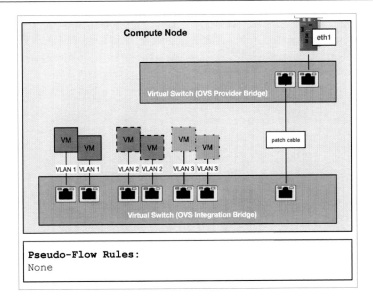

In the preceding diagram, instances in the same local VLAN are able to communicate with one another. The lack of flow rules for those virtual switch ports means that traffic from those ports is isolated to the virtual switch and will not be forwarded to the provider bridge and onto the physical network infrastructure. The inability of instances connected to local networks to communicate with instances and services on other hosts or networks means that local networks are not very useful in production and are recommended for testing purposes only.

Flat networks

A **flat network** in Neutron is analogous to an untagged network. This means that Neutron does not tag the traffic as it leaves a virtual switch and hits the physical network. Since the traffic is untagged, the physical switch port must be configured as an access or untagged port, or a native (default) VLAN should be used if the port is configured as a trunk or tagged port. A consequence of this configuration is that only a single flat network can exist per bridge and corresponding physical interface.

On a host using the `LinuxBridge` driver, when a flat network is created, an untagged interface is attached to the virtual switch or bridge. The following diagram shows these connections:

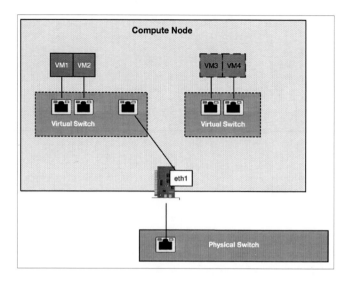

In the preceding diagram, `eth1` is connected directly to the virtual switch on the left. Traffic in and out of the bridge is untagged. The main `eth1` interface cannot be connected to any other bridge, but tagged sub-interfaces off `eth1` may be connected to other virtual switches. This will be demonstrated when we look at VLAN networks.

Using the `brctl show` command, we can see how a single flat network is represented on the host:

```
# brctl show
bridge name      bridge id        STP enabled      interfaces
brqXXXXXX        <MAC Address>  no              VM1
                                                 VM2
                                                 eth1
```

With Open vSwitch and flat networks, we can begin to see how flow rules are used to manipulate traffic as it traverses the virtual switches. Each flat network corresponds to a local VLAN on each host. In the following diagram, local **VLAN 1** corresponds to a flat Neutron network:

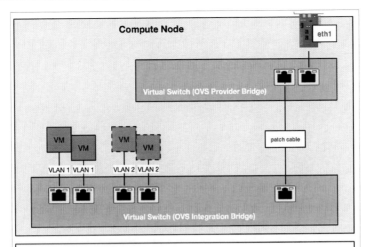

```
Pseudo-Flow Rules:

OUTBOUND: As traffic from VLAN 1 leaves the
integration bridge, strip the VLAN tag and drop on
eth1 untagged.

INBOUND: As untagged traffic enters eth1 towards
the integration bridge, add a VLAN tag of 1 and
forward to the appropriate VM.
```

In the preceding diagram, outbound traffic from a virtual machine instance connected to the integration bridge in **VLAN 1** will have its local VLAN tag stripped as it traverses the virtual switches and goes into the physical network. The physical switch will treat the traffic as untagged and forward the traffic accordingly to other devices in the network. Likewise, as untagged traffic enters the provider bridge from the physical network, OVS will add a VLAN tag of **1** and forward it to the appropriate host in **VLAN 1** on the integration bridge. The Open vSwitch agent on each node is responsible for programming flow rules based on the information in the Neutron database and the local OVS database.

VLAN networks

A **VLAN network** in Neutron is analogous to a tagged network. This means that Neutron will tag the traffic as it leaves a virtual switch and hits the physical network. Since the traffic is tagged, the physical switch port connected to the server's interface must be configured as a trunk port.

On a host using the `LinuxBridge` driver, when a VLAN network is created, a tagged interface is attached to the virtual switch or bridge, as shown in the following diagram:

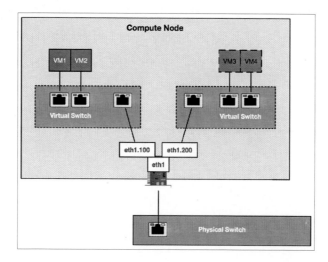

In the preceding diagram, the sub-interface `eth1.100` is connected to the virtual switch on the left. As traffic leaves the bridge, a VLAN tag of *100* is added to each packet and it is sent out `eth1` to the physical network. Likewise, as tagged traffic enters the `eth1` interface and respective virtual switch from the physical network, the kernel strips the tag and forwards the traffic to the appropriate virtual machine instance connected to the bridge.

Using the `brctl show` command, we can see how a VLAN network is represented on a host:

```
# brctl show
bridge name      bridge id         STP enabled     interfaces
brqXXXXXX        <MAC Address>     no              VM1
                                                   VM2
                                                   eth1.100
brqYYYYYY        <MAC Address>     no              VM3
                                                   VM4
                                                   eth1.200
```

With Open vSwitch and VLAN networks, every real VLAN corresponds to a local VLAN on each host. In the following diagram, local **VLAN 1** corresponds to real VLAN **100**, and local **VLAN 2** corresponds to real VLAN **200**:

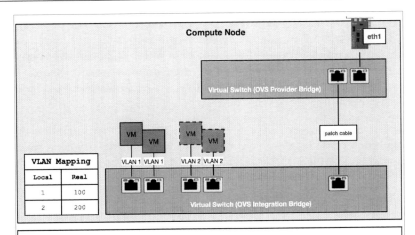

Pseudo-Flow Rules:

OUTBOUND: As traffic from VLAN 1 leaves the integration bridge, change the VLAN tag from 1 to 100 and forward out eth1.

INBOUND: As traffic tagged as VLAN 100 enters eth1 towards the integration bridge, change the VLAN tag from 100 to 1 and forward to the appropriate VM.

In the preceding diagram, outbound traffic from a virtual machine instance connected to the integration bridge in **VLAN 1** will have its VLAN tag modified as it traverses the virtual switches and enters the physical network. The physical switch will treat the traffic as tagged and forward it accordingly. Likewise, as tagged traffic enters the provider bridge from the physical network, OVS will modify the real VLAN ID to the local VLAN ID and forward the traffic to the appropriate host connected to the integration bridge.

VXLAN networks

Virtual eXtensible Local Area Network (VXLAN), is an overlay network technology that helps address scalability issues seen with VLANs. Where the maximum number of VLAN networks is *4,096* for a single switching layer, up to 16 million VXLAN networks can exist per **VXLAN Tunnel End Point (VTEP)**. VXLAN encapsulates **Layer 2 Ethernet** frames inside **Layer 4 UDP** packets that can be forwarded or routed between hosts. This means that a virtual network can be transparently extended across a large network, such as the Internet, without any changes to the end hosts. However, in the case of Neutron, a VXLAN mesh network is commonly constructed only between infrastructure nodes that exist in the same general location.

Rather than using VLAN IDs to differentiate networks, VXLAN uses a **VXLAN Network Identifier (VNI)** to function as the unique network identifier on a link that potentially carries traffic for tens of thousands, or millions, of different networks. With Neutron, virtual machine instances are unaware that VXLAN is used to connect traffic between hosts. The VTEP on the physical node handles the encapsulation and decapsulation of traffic without the instance ever knowing.

On a host using the `LinuxBridge` driver, when a Neutron VXLAN network is created, an interface is created on each host and is responsible for encapsulating and decapsulating traffic for that particular network:

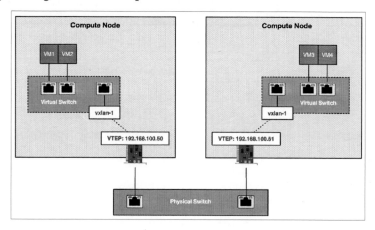

In the preceding diagram, the virtual interface `vxlan-1` is connected to the virtual switch. Created by Neutron, the `vxlan-1` interface is tied to the interface configured with the VTEP address. As traffic leaves the bridge, the `vxlan-1` interface encapsulates the traffic within a UDP packet and forwards it out the physical network to the other compute node's VTEP address, `192.168.100.51`, where the traffic is decapsulated and forwarded to the respective virtual machine instance.

Using the `brctl show` command, we can see how a VXLAN network is represented on a host:

```
# brctl show
bridge name      bridge id        STP enabled     interfaces
brqXXXXXX        <MAC Address>    no              VM1
                                                  VM2
                                                  vxlan-1
```

With Open vSwitch, the process of encapsulating and decapsulating VXLAN traffic is accomplished with flow rules rather than virtual interfaces. Neutron implements a dedicated virtual switch for overlay traffic, known as the **tunnel bridge**.

The tunnel bridge connects the integration bridge to the overlay network that exists between VTEPs rather than the physical network, like the provider bridge does. In the following diagram, traffic from **VM1** on **Compute Node A** to **VM2** on **Compute Node B** is forwarded over the overlay network:

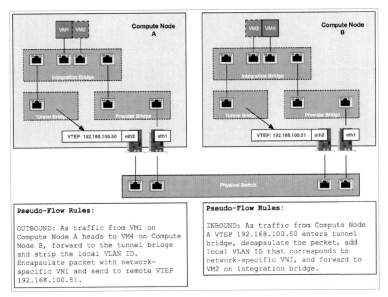

In the preceding diagram, each host has a VTEP that is used for VXLAN overlay network traffic. Traffic between virtual machine instances in VXLAN networks on different hosts is all forwarded through the same tunnel endpoint and differentiated by VNIs that correspond to each Neutron network. OVS agents on each host keep track of the VNI-to-local VLAN mappings and maintain the flow rules that ensure traffic gets forwarded appropriately.

While not as well-performing as VLAN or flat networks on certain hardware, the use of VXLAN is becoming more popular in cloud network architectures, where scalability and self service are major drivers.

GRE networks

A **GRE network** is similar to a VXLAN network in that traffic from one instance to another is encapsulated and sent over an existing **Layer 3** network. A unique segmentation ID is used to differentiate traffic from other GRE networks. Rather than use UDP as the transport mechanism, GRE traffic uses IP protocol 47. For various reasons, including performance, the use of GRE for encapsulating tenant network traffic has fallen out of favor now that VXLAN is supported by both Open vSwitch and LinuxBridge network driver.

More information on how GRE encapsulation works is described in RFC 2784, available at https://tools.ietf.org/html/rfc2784.

 As of the Liberty release of OpenStack, the LinuxBridge driver does not implement GRE networks.

A look at our environment

In the previous chapter, we created multiple Neutron networks that launched a series of automated events, including:

- The creation of network namespaces
- The startup of DHCP services for each network
- The connecting of each namespace to the virtual switch
- The configuration of virtual switch ports

The following commands are useful in seeing how the virtual network infrastructure is represented on the host:

Command	Purpose
`ovs-vsctl show`	Shows all virtual switches on the host
`ovs-vsctl dump-flows <bridge>`	Shows the flow rules for the specified bridge
`ovs-vsctl add-br <bridge>`	Creates a virtual switch
`ovs-vsctl add-port <bridge> <interface>`	Adds an interface to a virtual switch
`ovs-vsctl list-ports <bridge>`	Lists the ports of a virtual switch
`ovs-ofctl show <bridge>`	Lists the ports of a virtual switch with details

 There is a lot of useful information for each of these commands hidden in their respective man pages. Use the man `<command>` command to find out more.

Getting a closer look

As the admin user, let's use the Neutron `net-list` and `net-show` commands from the CLI to review the details of the networks we created in the previous chapter:

```
[root@allinone ~]# source keystonerc_admin
[root@allinone ~(keystone_admin)]# neutron net-list
+--------------------------------------+----------------+------------------------------------------------------+
| id                                   | name           | subnets                                              |
+--------------------------------------+----------------+------------------------------------------------------+
| c8cde907-9a30-4e86-8c31-11d11f56cb2c | MyDemoNetwork  | 6ee10d34-4d82-4901-9627-22a758096e52 192.168.8.0/24  |
| 460b2688-02c4-42db-b25c-7e9ba749d368 | MySimpleNetwork| 04c12ff9-380d-4a4e-a8aa-f31536406ad4 192.168.1.0/24  |
+--------------------------------------+----------------+------------------------------------------------------+
```

Using the Neutron `net-show` command, take a look at the details of each network:

```
[root@allinone ~(keystone_admin)]# neutron net-show MyDemoNetwork
+---------------------------+--------------------------------------+
| Field                     | Value                                |
+---------------------------+--------------------------------------+
| admin_state_up            | True                                 |
| id                        | c8cde907-9a30-4e86-8c31-11d11f56cb2c |
| mtu                       | 0                                    |
| name                      | MyDemoNetwork                        |
| provider:network_type     | vxlan                                |
| provider:physical_network |                                      |
| provider:segmentation_id  | 38                                   |
| router:external           | False                                |
| shared                    | False                                |
| status                    | ACTIVE                               |
| subnets                   | 6ee10d34-4d82-4901-9627-22a758096e52 |
| tenant_id                 | b8e0562dab644c87aa693abf48d3040d     |
+---------------------------+--------------------------------------+

[root@allinone ~(keystone_admin)]# neutron net-show MySimpleNetwork
+---------------------------+--------------------------------------+
| Field                     | Value                                |
+---------------------------+--------------------------------------+
| admin_state_up            | True                                 |
| id                        | 460b2688-02c4-42db-b25c-7e9ba749d368 |
| mtu                       | 0                                    |
| name                      | MySimpleNetwork                      |
| provider:network_type     | vxlan                                |
| provider:physical_network |                                      |
| provider:segmentation_id  | 99                                   |
| router:external           | False                                |
| shared                    | False                                |
| status                    | ACTIVE                               |
| subnets                   | 04c12ff9-380d-4a4e-a8aa-f31536406ad4 |
| tenant_id                 | c51a93428ada44f297e5fe65a3ac3b9f     |
+---------------------------+--------------------------------------+
```

In the output, we can see that the network `MyDemoNetwork` is a VXLAN network with a segmentation ID of 38. The other network, `MySimpleNetwork`, is also a VXLAN network, but with a segmentation ID of 99. Both segmentation IDs were chosen by Neutron at random and will be different in your environment.

 The segmentation ID of a VXLAN network is synonymous with the VNI used when encapsulating the packet.

Using the `ovs-vsctl show` command, we can see the virtual switches configured on the host:

```
[root@allinone ~(keystone_admin)]# ovs-vsctl show
3295ca6c-23cf-4b55-9ed8-f5e1e6c39a30
    Bridge br-ex
        Port br-ex
            Interface br-ex
                type: internal
        Port "enp0s8"
            Interface "enp0s8"
        Port phy-br-ex
            Interface phy-br-ex
                type: patch
                options: {peer=int-br-ex}
    Bridge br-tun
        fail_mode: secure
        Port br-tun
            Interface br-tun
                type: internal
        Port patch-int
            Interface patch-int
                type: patch
                options: {peer=patch-tun}
    Bridge br-int
        fail_mode: secure
        Port br-int
            Interface br-int
                type: internal
        Port int-br-ex
            Interface int-br-ex
                type: patch
                options: {peer=phy-br-ex}
        Port patch-tun
            Interface patch-tun
                type: patch
                options: {peer=patch-int}
        Port "tap94c668d7-5a"
            tag: 1
            Interface "tap94c668d7-5a"
                type: internal
        Port "tap9a237a63-df"
            tag: 2
            Interface "tap9a237a63-df"
                type: internal
    ovs_version: "2.4.0"
```

The first switch listed, `br-ex`, is the provider bridge that is connected to the physical network:

```
Bridge br-ex
    Port br-ex
        Interface br-ex
            type: internal
    Port "enp0s8"
        Interface "enp0s8"
    Port phy-br-ex
        Interface phy-br-ex
            type: patch
            options: {peer=int-br-ex}
```

In this example, the provider bridge is connected to the `enp0s8` interface of the host. In most cases, provider bridges across hosts in the cloud will be connected to one another through the physical infrastructure.

On a real server, the enp0s8 interface would likely be connected to a switch port configured as a `trunk` and capable of handling tagged traffic. For the purposes of this book, the interface should be considered untagged.

The next switch, `br-tun`, is the tunnel bridge that establishes the overlay network between hosts:

```
Bridge br-tun
    fail_mode: secure
    Port br-tun
        Interface br-tun
            type: internal
    Port patch-int
        Interface patch-int
            type: patch
            options: {peer=patch-tun}
```

Last but not least, the integration bridge, `br-int`, is connected to all virtual network devices on the host and cross-connected to the provider and tunnel bridges:

```
Bridge br-int
    fail_mode: secure
    Port br-int
        Interface br-int
            type: internal
    Port int-br-ex
        Interface int-br-ex
            type: patch
            options: {peer=phy-br-ex}
    Port patch-tun
        Interface patch-tun
            type: patch
            options: {peer=patch-int}
    Port "tap94c668d7-5a"
        tag: 1
        Interface "tap94c668d7-5a"
            type: internal
    Port "tap9a237a63-df"
        tag: 2
        Interface "tap9a237a63-df"
            type: internal
```

Take a look at the last two ports listed: `tap94c668d7-5a` and `tap9a237a63-df`. Each of these virtual switch ports corresponds to a logical Neutron port that is connected to some virtual device. In this example, the two ports correspond to the two DHCP servers living in network namespaces that were created automatically when we created `MyDemoNetwork` and `MySimpleNetworks` in the previous chapter.

These virtual switches and their connections are represented in the following diagram:

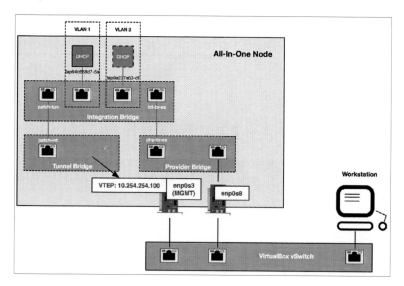

In this environment, the tunnel bridge will go unused since there is only one host. As we continue to build the environment in the following chapters, the diagram will be updated to show connections to Neutron routers and virtual machine instances.

Summary

In this chapter, we covered the two most popular open source virtual switching platforms for OpenStack, known as Open vSwitch and LinuxBridge. If you're an ordinary user without access to the underlying infrastructure, much of what has been covered and represented in this chapter will not be directly observable by you. For administrators and operators, though, understanding how the virtual switching infrastructure interacts with the physical infrastructure is crucial to understanding, operating, and supporting OpenStack clouds. In the next chapter, we will take a look at how Neutron implements virtual routers that provide routing between Neutron networks. Concepts that will be covered include network namespaces, **Source Network Address Translation (SNAT)**, and floating IPs.

6

Routing

In the previous chapter, we discovered how Neutron builds out logical networks using two of the most popular open source virtual switching platforms for OpenStack: Open vSwitch and LinuxBridge. In this chapter, we will take a look at how Neutron implements virtual routers that provide routing between Neutron networks and the outside world. Concepts that will be covered include network namespaces, **Source Network Address Translation (SNAT)**, and floating IPs.

The basics of routing in Neutron

If you recall from the previous chapter, users can create and manage networks known as **tenant networks** within their respective project without any knowledge of the underlying infrastructure. By default, instances connected to tenant networks are isolated from other networks and are unable to access external resources such as the Internet. Neutron provides connectivity to instances in tenant networks by way of virtual routers.

Network namespaces

In a reference implementation, virtual routers created in Neutron are implemented as network namespaces that reside on nodes running the Neutron L3 agent service. Network namespaces are similar in function to **Virtual Routing and Forwarding (VRF)** domains, where multiple instances of a routing table exist to provide complete network segregation in a single device. The use of network namespaces allows Neutron to support overlapping subnets across networks. In Linux, network namespaces can be managed using the `ip netns` command as the `root` user or a user with `sudo` privileges. Router namespaces follow the `qrouter-<router_id>` naming convention.

In addition to providing dedicated routing tables to each namespace, Linux allows processes like `dnsmasq` to be run and contained within namespaces. Neutron uses network namespaces to isolate DHCP services between networks. DHCP namespaces follow the `qdhcp-<network_id>` naming convention.

The Neutron L3 agent service usually runs on controller nodes or dedicated network nodes, but as we'll see later, the service can also run on compute nodes to help provide a smaller failure zone when using distributed virtual routers.

Connectivity through a router

At its most basic level, a Neutron router acts as a `default` gateway for one or more connected tenant networks, as shown in the following diagram:

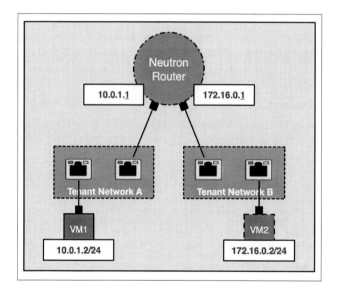

Instances in **Tenant Network A** can use the Neutron router as their `default` gateway to communicate with instances in **Tenant Network B**, and vice versa. When an external provider network is attached to the Neutron router, the router can route traffic upstream to its respective gateway device. In most cases, a physical routing device will be the gateway for a Neutron router. The following diagram demonstrates a physical gateway and the Neutron router connected to a common provider network:

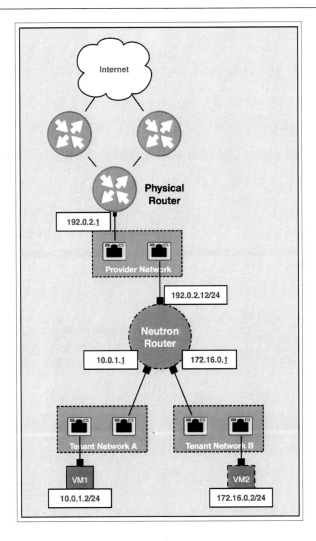

In the diagram, a Neutron router is connected to multiple tenant networks and serves as the `default` gateway for those networks. The Neutron router is also connected to a provider network that provides access to external networks, including the Internet.

Outbound connectivity

By default, Neutron routers will apply **Source Network Address Translation** (**SNAT**) to all outbound traffic from connected tenant networks. This means that, as traffic exits the virtual router and heads upstream, the router modifies each packet and changes the source IP address to that of its own external interface. This ensures that return traffic gets directed back to the virtual router, where the destination IP address is modified from the router's address back to the original client. The following diagram demonstrates a router performing SNAT for a virtual machine instance:

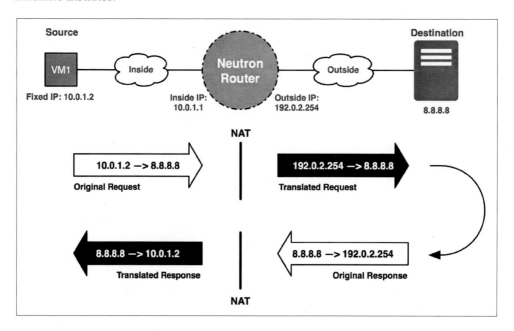

In the diagram, the outbound traffic from **VM 1** is modified as it traverses the Neutron router towards its destination. As each packet leaves the router, the source address is modified. As the inbound response traffic enters and traverses the router, the destination address is changed from that of the router to that of the virtual machine.

Inbound connectivity

In a SNAT scenario, all traffic leaving the router appears to come from the same address. In addition, inbound connections cannot be made directly to a SNAT address, which means that that address cannot be used to reach the instance directly.

A floating IP is an address that is used to provide a 1:1 static NAT mapping to a single fixed IP. In Nova/Neutron-speak, a fixed IP is an IP address associated with an instance and, by definition, a Neutron port. Floating IPs provide a unique outbound and inbound address; this allows clients to reach individual virtual machine instances and other devices. The following diagram demonstrates a router performing an address translation using a floating IP:

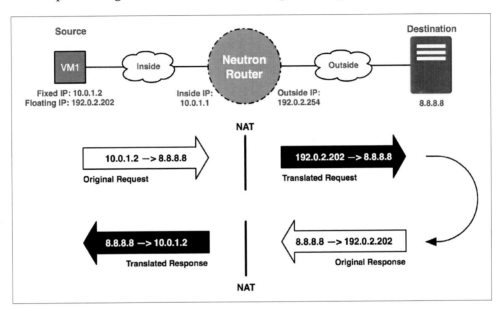

In the diagram, the outbound traffic from **VM 1** is modified as it traverses the Neutron router towards its destination. As each packet leaves the router, the source address is modified to that of the floating IP. As the inbound response traffic enters and traverses the router, the destination address is changed from that of the router to that of the virtual machine. This is similar in operation to the earlier SNAT example. Rather than using a shared address, however, the floating IP is dedicated to traffic associated with the fixed IP of the instance. Inbound connections to the floating IP from an external network are translated to the respective fixed IP and directed to the appropriate resource or instance.

Types of routers

Neutron routers act as the `default` gateway for connected tenant networks and provide outbound and inbound connectivity to the instances they service. Neutron provides three types of routers to users:

- Standalone
- Highly available
- Distributed

Routers can be created in both the **Horizon** dashboard and via the Neutron CLI. As an ordinary user, the type of router that is created via the API is predetermined, based on a combination of settings found in the Neutron server and L3 agent configuration files. Users with the `admin` role are free to define the type of router to be created using the `router-create` command, using the following flags:

```
--distributed {true | false}
--ha {true | false}
```

Neutron does not expose the router type to users via the API, even with the `router-show` command. Users with the `admin` role, however, can see those details. The **Horizon** dashboard limits all users, including administrative users, to the `default` router type specified in the configuration. This behavior may change in future releases.

Standalone routers

A **standalone router** is a single logical router that is implemented as a single network namespace on a host running the Neutron L3 agent. Most often, the L3 agent runs on dedicated network nodes or the controller nodes themselves. By its very nature, a standalone router is a single point of failure for directly connected networks. If the node hosting the network namespace experiences issues, connectivity through the namespace can become limited or completely unavailable. Needless to say, the failure of a standalone router can result in an unhappy user experience.

Standalone routers have been the `default` router type since the Folsom release of OpenStack and are supported by both the Open vSwitch and LinuxBridge mechanism drivers and agents.

Highly available routers

A **Highly Available (HA)** router is a single logical router that is implemented as two or more network namespaces on hosts running the Neutron L3 agent. Like its standalone counterpart, an HA router is likely to be spread across dedicated network or controller nodes. An HA router utilizes the `keepalived` service and the **Virtual Routing Redundancy Protocol (VRRP)** between network namespaces to provide high availability. Only one of the network namespaces acts as a master virtual router at any given time while the others remain in a backup state awaiting a failover event. If the active router fails, a backup router will take over quickly. While HA routers provide redundancy not found with standalone routers, pushing all traffic through a subset of nodes may still be seen as a bottleneck that can result in poor network performance.

Highly available routers have been available since the Juno release of OpenStack and are supported by both the Open vSwitch and LinuxBridge mechanism drivers and agents.

Distributed virtual routers

A **Distributed Virtual Router (DVR)** is a single logical router that is implemented as multiple network namespaces on network and compute nodes. The model of distributing virtual routers across compute nodes is similar to the multihost functionality of **Nova Network**. It offers high availability of networking by limiting single points of failure to individual compute nodes rather than network nodes.

Distributed virtual routers have been available since the Juno release of OpenStack and, as of the Liberty release, are supported only by the Open vSwitch mechanism driver and agent.

> Highly available and distributed virtual routers require the use of more than one host and won't be created as part of the exercises demonstrated in this book. For a more in-depth look at HA and distributed virtual routers, check out *Learning OpenStack Networking (Neutron), Second Edition,* available through Packt Publishing at `https://www.packtpub.com/virtualization-and-cloud/learning-openstack-networking-neutron-second-edition`.

Managing routers in the dashboard

Like networks, virtual routers can be created and managed within the **Horizon** dashboard and by using the Neutron command-line client.

Creating routers within a project

To create a router, follow these steps:

1. Navigate to the **Project** | **Network** | **Routers** section of the **Horizon** dashboard and click on the **Create Router** button in the upper right-hand corner of the screen, as shown here:

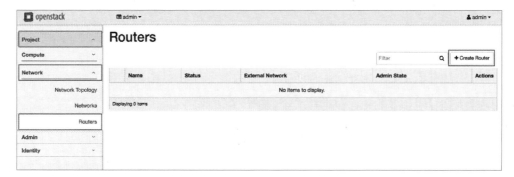

2. A single-step router creation wizard will appear. Name the router in the **Router Name** field, as shown here:

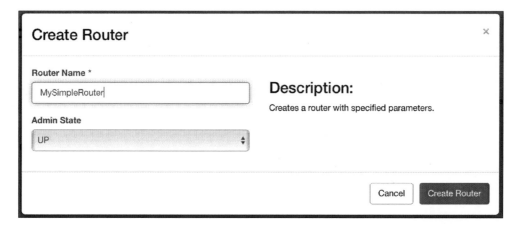

3. Click on the **Create Router** button to complete the wizard and return to the **Routers** screen, as shown in the following screenshot:

Congratulations, you just created a virtual router! Behind the scenes, Neutron has determined the type of router to create and may have implemented one or more network namespaces as a result. In this environment, the `default` router type is `standalone`, which means a single network namespace will be created that will serve as the virtual router. In *Chapter 7, Building Networks and Routers*, we'll build some common network topologies and observe traffic flow through a Neutron router.

Viewing the network topology

Now that we have created a router, let's view the resulting network topology. Here are the steps:

1. From the **Project | Network** menu, choose **Network Topology**:

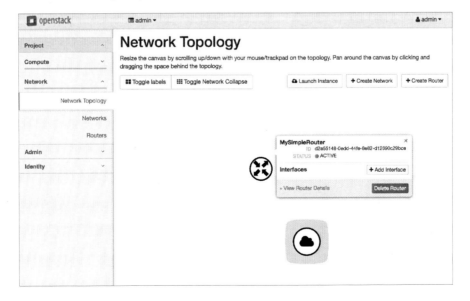

2. Right now, the topology consists of a single network object and a single router object. Notice that the router and network are not connected. To connect the router to the network, click on the **Add Interface** button, shown here:

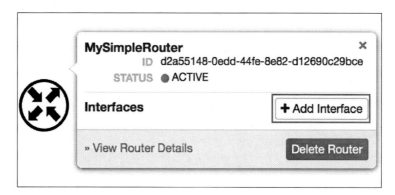

3. An interface wizard will appear. From the **Subnet** menu, select the subnet to attach the router to:

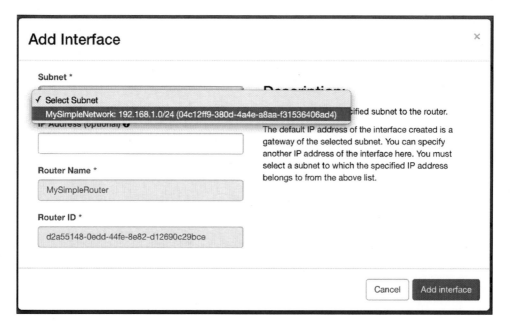

4. When adding an interface to a router, the router will take on the IP address defined in the `gateway_ip` attribute of the selected subnet. Instead, you can specify a different IP in the **IP Address** field. Click on the **Add interface** button to complete the wizard and return to the network topology screen pictured here:

The router is now connected to the network! This means that an instance in the `MySimpleNetwork` network can use the router as its `default` gateway.

 Additional interfaces can be added to the router, but only from other networks. A Neutron router should not be connected to the same network more than once.

Managing routers as an administrator

From the **Admin | System | Routers** window, administrators can view all routers in the cloud as well as edit and delete selected routers, as shown here:

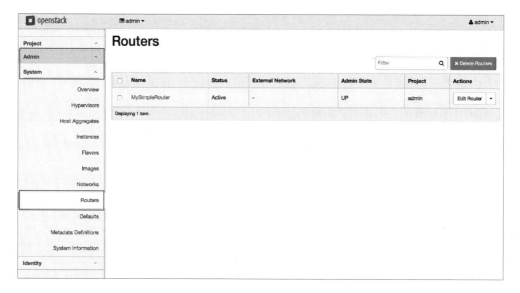

Here, we can see the previously created router, `MySimpleRouter`. Clicking on the router name provides a limited subset of the actions that are available through the **Project | Network | Routers** pane:

Administrators can only delete routers, mark their administrative state **UP** or **DOWN**, view static routes, and add or delete interfaces. All other router management functions must be done from within the respective **Project** panel.

Managing routers with the Neutron client

The Neutron command-line client provides additional functionality not found in the **Horizon** dashboard, including the ability to specify the type of router to create.

Creating and listing routers

Listing networks with the Neutron client is as easy as using the neutron router-list command, shown here:

```
[root@allinone ~(keystone_admin)]# neutron router-list
+--------------------------------------+--------------+---------------------+-------------+-------+
| id                                   | name         | external_gateway_info | distributed | ha    |
+--------------------------------------+--------------+---------------------+-------------+-------+
| d2a55148-0edd-44fe-8e82-d12690c29bce | MySimpleRouter | null              | False       | False |
+--------------------------------------+--------------+---------------------+-------------+-------+
```

Running the router-list command as an administrator will return all routers known to Neutron, while running the command as an ordinary user will only return routers associated with the user's tenant or project. As an example, let's authenticate as the demo user and run the same command to see what is returned:

```
[root@allinone ~(keystone_admin)]# source keystonerc_demo
[root@allinone ~(keystone_demo)]# neutron router-list

[root@allinone ~(keystone_demo)]#
```

As expected, no routers were returned. Routers, like other OpenStack resources, are associated with a single tenant or project and can only be viewed or managed by the respective users of those projects or by administrators.

Creating a router

Creating a router with the Neutron client can be accomplished with the neutron router-create command. In this example, the demo user is logged in and the router to be created is named MyDemoRouter:

```
[root@allinone ~(keystone_demo)]# neutron router-create MyDemoRouter
```

The operation returns a response that can be seen in the following output:

```
Created a new router:
+------------------------+-----------------------------------------+
| Field                  | Value                                   |
+------------------------+-----------------------------------------+
| admin_state_up         | True                                    |
| external_gateway_info  |                                         |
| id                     | dfa617ad-3ded-4962-9484-a5e9ce138172    |
| name                   | MyDemoRouter                            |
| routes                 |                                         |
| status                 | ACTIVE                                  |
| tenant_id              | b8e0562dab644c87aa693abf48d3040d        |
+------------------------+-----------------------------------------+
```

Notice that the output did not return information regarding the router type. As an ordinary user, that information is not exposed by Neutron and is only available to users with the admin role.

Copy the id and name values from the output. You will use the router ID when you add an interface to the router or perform certain other network activities. In some cases, the router name can be used in lieu of the ID, but only when the name is unique. In this example, the ID is dfa617ad-3ded-4962-9484-a5e9ce138172, but the value will be unique in your response.

Adding an interface

Adding an interface to a router with the Neutron client can be accomplished with the neutron router-interface-add command. To add an interface, you must specify the router and subnet name or ID.

> Users who consume all available addresses in a subnet may find it necessary to add additional subnets to a network. Neutron allows multiple subnets to be associated with a single network, and routers should be connected to each subnet using the router-interface-add command.

If you recall from *Chapter 4, Interfacing with Neutron*, we created a network and subnet as the demo user, named MyDemoNetwork and MyDemoSubnet, respectively. As the demo user, perform a neutron net-list command to retrieve a list of networks and associated subnets, like this:

```
[root@allinone ~(keystone_demo)]# neutron net-list
+--------------------------------------+--------------+----------------------------------------------+
| id                                   | name         | subnets                                      |
+--------------------------------------+--------------+----------------------------------------------+
| c8cde907-9a30-4e86-8c31-11d11f56cb2c | MyDemoNetwork| 6ee10d34-4d82-4901-9627-22a758096e52 192.168.8.0/24 |
+--------------------------------------+--------------+----------------------------------------------+
```

Using the neutron router-interface-add command, add an interface to the router and attach it to the MyDemoSubnet subnet:

```
[root@allinone ~(keystone_demo)]# neutron router-interface-add MyDemoRouter MyDemoSubnet
Added interface 9fff8744-fd64-4e34-b55b-ecd9ff402eba to router MyDemoRouter.
```

That's it! As a result of adding an interface to the router via the API, Neutron created a logical Neutron port for the virtual network interface used by the router, created the virtual interface inside the respective network namespace, attached the interface to the virtual switch or bridge, and configured an IP address on the virtual interface that corresponds with the address defined by the gateway_ip attribute of the subnet. Thanks, Neutron!

Listing router interfaces

To obtain a list of the Neutron ports associated with a router, use the neutron router-port-list command, seen here:

```
[root@allinone ~(keystone_demo)]# neutron router-port-list MyDemoRouter
+--------------------------------------+------+-------------------+------------------------------------------------------------------------------------+
| id                                   | name | mac_address       | fixed_ips                                                                          |
+--------------------------------------+------+-------------------+------------------------------------------------------------------------------------+
| 9fff8744-fd64-4e34-b55b-ecd9ff402eba |      | fa:16:3e:86:50:2b | {"subnet_id": "6ee10d34-4d82-4901-9627-22a758096e52", "ip_address": "192.168.8.1"} |
+--------------------------------------+------+-------------------+------------------------------------------------------------------------------------+
```

All ports currently associated with the router will be listed in the output. As expected, the fixed IP of the port corresponds to the gateway_ip of the MyDemoSubnet subnet.

Examining the routers

Virtual routers are implemented as network namespaces on one or more nodes. In our single-node environment, the two routers that have been created so far can both be found on the same node. Using the `ip netns` command as `root` or a user with `sudo` privileges, you can list all network namespaces on a host, like so:

```
[root@allinone ~(keystone_admin)]# ip netns
qrouter-dfa617ad-3ded-4962-9484-a5e9ce138172
qrouter-d2a55148-0edd-44fe-8e82-d12690c29bce
qdhcp-460b2688-02c4-42db-b25c-7e9ba749d368
qdhcp-c8cde907-9a30-4e86-8c31-11d11f56cb2c
```

The two `qrouter` namespaces in the list correspond to the two routers we've created so far:

```
[root@allinone ~(keystone_admin)]# neutron router-list
+--------------------------------------+----------------+----------------------+-------------+-------+
| id                                   | name           | external_gateway_info | distributed | ha    |
+--------------------------------------+----------------+----------------------+-------------+-------+
| d2a55148-0edd-44fe-8e82-d12690c29bce | MySimpleRouter | null                 | False       | False |
| dfa617ad-3ded-4962-9484-a5e9ce138172 | MyDemoRouter   | null                 | False       | False |
+--------------------------------------+----------------+----------------------+-------------+-------+
```

Using the `ip netns exec <namespace>` command, you can specify a command to execute within the specified namespace. Useful commands such as `ip`, `netstat`, `ps`, and `iptables` provide details within the scope of the namespace they're executed in. A quick look at the `MySimpleRouter` network namespace shows the virtual interface created by Neutron when we attached the router to the `MySimpleSubnet` subnet earlier in this chapter:

```
[root@allinone ~(keystone_admin)]# ip netns exec qrouter-d2a55148-0edd-44fe-8e82-d12690c29bce ip a
1: lo: <LOOPBACK,UP,LOWER_UP> mtu 65536 qdisc noqueue state UNKNOWN
    link/loopback 00:00:00:00:00:00 brd 00:00:00:00:00:00
    inet 127.0.0.1/8 scope host lo
       valid_lft forever preferred_lft forever
    inet6 ::1/128 scope host
       valid_lft forever preferred_lft forever
14: qr-2e525501-5f: <BROADCAST,MULTICAST,UP,LOWER_UP> mtu 1500 qdisc noqueue state UNKNOWN
    link/ether fa:16:3e:c5:b6:d8 brd ff:ff:ff:ff:ff:ff
    inet 192.168.1.1/24 brd 192.168.1.255 scope global qr-2e525501-5f
       valid_lft forever preferred_lft forever
    inet6 fe80::f816:3eff:fec5:b6d8/64 scope link
       valid_lft forever preferred_lft forever
```

Using the `ovs-vsctl` show command, we can see the `qr-2e525501-5f` interface attached to the integration bridge in a local VLAN mapped to `MySimpleNetwork`:

```
[root@allinone ~(keystone_admin)]# ovs-vsctl show
3295ca6c-23cf-4b55-9ed8-f5e1e6c39a30
    Bridge br-ex
        <snip>
    Bridge br-tun
        <snip>
    Bridge br-int
        fail_mode: secure
        Port br-int
            Interface br-int
                type: internal
        Port "qr-2e525501-5f"
            tag: 1
            Interface "qr-2e525501-5f"
                type: internal
        Port "tap9a237a63-df"
            tag: 2
            Interface "tap9a237a63-df"
                type: internal
        Port int-br-ex
            Interface int-br-ex
                type: patch
                options: {peer=phy-br-ex}
        Port "qr-9fff8744-fd"
            tag: 2
            Interface "qr-9fff8744-fd"
                type: internal
        Port patch-tun
            Interface patch-tun
                type: patch
                options: {peer=patch-int}
        Port "tap94c668d7-5a"
            tag: 1
            Interface "tap94c668d7-5a"
                type: internal
    ovs_version: "2.4.0"
```

Additional router interfaces will be connected to the same integration bridge, but they will be tagged with different local VLAN tags and names based on the network, subnet, and port the interfaces are associated with.

Summary

In this chapter, we learned that Neutron routers can route between directly connected tenant networks and external networks using network address translation. Neutron routers can be configured in a redundant or distributed manner, and they trade simplicity in their implementation for high availability. Like the virtual switching infrastructure covered in the previous chapter, users without access to the underlying infrastructure will be unable to observe how Neutron implements virtual routers and their respective features. The logical network diagram provided within the Horizon dashboard, coupled with an understanding of the concepts outlined in this book, will help you understand what is happening behind the scenes.

In the next chapter, we will take a look at some common virtual network architectures that can be built by users and will showcase the traffic flow from client workstations to virtual machine instances using floating IPs.

7
Building Networks and Routers

In the previous chapter, we learned that Neutron routers provide connectivity between user-created tenant networks and external networks such as the Internet using network address translation. In this chapter, we will take a look at some basic virtual network architectures and will showcase the traffic flow from client workstation to virtual machine instance via fixed and floating IPs.

Basic network architectures and functions that will be covered include:

- Single-homed instances connected to provider networks
- Single-homed instances behind Neutron routers
- Source NAT
- Floating IP

So sit back, get comfortable, and let's take a look at some networks and routers.

Using provider networks

If you recall from *Chapter 3, Neutron API Basics*, administrators, or users with the `admin` role, can create and manage networks known as provider networks that map a logical Neutron network to a physical network in the data center. Creating a provider network requires knowledge of the physical infrastructure, such as 802.1q VLAN IDs and server interfaces used to forward traffic.

Connecting instances to provider networks gives users the ability to access their instances directly by their fixed IP addresses with no hops through a virtual router. The following logical diagram represents a virtual machine instance connected to a provider network:

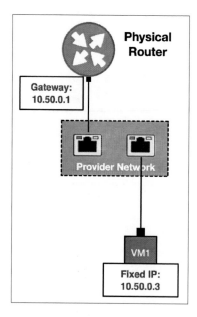

In the diagram, an instance is directly accessible from the upstream router via its fixed IP address. The fixed IP address is the address configured within the virtual machine. The compute node bridges the physical and virtual network and allows the virtual machine instance to be in the same **Layer 2** broadcast domain and **Layer 3** network as the physical gateway device.

 The actual implementation of provider or tenant networks will vary between network drivers configured on the infrastructure nodes, but the logical model should be consistent between all of them.

Connecting instances directly to provider networks exposes instances directly to the physical network, so to speak. It can often result in higher performance compared to using overlay networking technologies, such as GRE or VXLAN, depending on the hardware used. One downside to this configuration, though, is that it limits users to using predefined networks and address space that may be better used for other purposes such as floating IPs, and it requires more administrative overhead.

Creating a provider network

Provider networks can be created using the `neutron net-create` command or from the **Horizon** dashboard within the **Admin | Networks** pane. Creating provider networks requires knowledge of the following network details:

- Network type
- Segmentation ID (if applicable to network type, for example, VLAN, VXLAN, or GRE)
- Physical interface mapping (if applicable to network type, for example, flat and VLAN)

 Based on the network infrastructure laid out in *Chapter 2, Installing OpenStack Using RDO*, we are limited to the creation of a single flat (untagged) provider network in this All-In-One environment.

Using the `neutron net-create` command, create a flat provider network named `MyExternalProviderNetwork` and map it to the `physnet1` interface, as shown in the following screenshot:

```
[root@allinone ~(keystone_admin)]# neutron net-create --provider:network_type=flat \
> --provider:physical_network=physnet1 MyExternalProviderNetwork

Created a new network:
+---------------------------+--------------------------------------+
| Field                     | Value                                |
+---------------------------+--------------------------------------+
| admin_state_up            | True                                 |
| id                        | 52550637-519f-496d-afd1-75ab7ff51e44 |
| mtu                       | 0                                    |
| name                      | MyExternalProviderNetwork            |
| provider:network_type     | flat                                 |
| provider:physical_network | physnet1                             |
| provider:segmentation_id  |                                      |
| router:external           | False                                |
| shared                    | False                                |
| status                    | ACTIVE                               |
| subnets                   |                                      |
| tenant_id                 | c51a93428ada44f297e5fe65a3ac3b9f     |
+---------------------------+--------------------------------------+
```

Remember, `physnet1` is just a label that represents a particular physical interface or bridge on the host. In this environment, `physnet1` maps to a bridge named `br-ex` that contains the interface `enp0s8`. The bridge `br-ex` is known as the **provider bridge**, since it is connected to the physical network by way of the connected interface. It is meant to bridge virtual and physical networks in an Open vSwitch-based environment.

Using the `neutron subnet-create` command, create a subnet and associate it with the `MyExternalProviderNetwork` network, as shown in the following screenshot:

```
[root@allinone ~(keystone_admin)]# neutron subnet-create MyExternalProviderNetwork 10.50.0.0/24 \
> --name=MyExternalProviderSubnet --gateway_ip=10.50.0.1

Created a new subnet:
+--------------------+-------------------------------------------------+
| Field              | Value                                           |
+--------------------+-------------------------------------------------+
| allocation_pools   | {"start": "10.50.0.2", "end": "10.50.0.254"}    |
| cidr               | 10.50.0.0/24                                     |
| dns_nameservers    |                                                 |
| enable_dhcp        | True                                            |
| gateway_ip         | 10.50.0.1                                        |
| host_routes        |                                                 |
| id                 | fe581964-41b0-42c6-b08e-b09ca254d631             |
| ip_version         | 4                                               |
| ipv6_address_mode  |                                                 |
| ipv6_ra_mode       |                                                 |
| name               | MyExternalProviderSubnet                         |
| network_id         | 52550637-519f-496d-afd1-75ab7ff51e44             |
| subnetpool_id      |                                                 |
| tenant_id          | c51a93428ada44f297e5fe65a3ac3b9f                 |
+--------------------+-------------------------------------------------+
```

The subnet we've defined, `10.50.0.0/24`, corresponds to a network created within VirtualBox that will allow us to access virtual machine instances and other OpenStack objects from our client workstation.

Booting an instance

To test the network, boot an instance using the `nova boot` command or the **Horizon** dashboard. Requirements for booting an instance include:

- Image
- Flavor

- Network interface (network or port ID)

- Name

 For simple connectivity tests, the CirrOS image has been included as part of the RDO installation. CirrOS is a free, lightweight Linux operating system.

The following screenshot shows an instance named `MyDirectInstance` booting on the `MyExternalProviderNetwork` network:

```
[root@allinone ~(keystone_admin)]# nova boot --image="cirros-0.3.4-x86_64" --flavor="m1.tiny" \
--nic net-id=52550637-519f-496d-afd1-75ab7ff51e44 MyDirectInstance
+-------------------------------------+-------------------------------------------------------+
| Property                            | Value                                                 |
+-------------------------------------+-------------------------------------------------------+
| OS-DCF:diskConfig                   | MANUAL                                                 |
| OS-EXT-AZ:availability_zone         |                                                       |
| OS-EXT-SRV-ATTR:host                | -                                                     |
| OS-EXT-SRV-ATTR:hypervisor_hostname | -                                                     |
| OS-EXT-SRV-ATTR:instance_name       | instance-00000002                                     |
| OS-EXT-STS:power_state              | 0                                                     |
| OS-EXT-STS:task_state               | scheduling                                            |
| OS-EXT-STS:vm_state                 | building                                              |
| OS-SRV-USG:launched_at              | -                                                     |
| OS-SRV-USG:terminated_at            | -                                                     |
| accessIPv4                          |                                                       |
| accessIPv6                          |                                                       |
| adminPass                           | h8pcM2pxLFr9                                           |
| config_drive                        |                                                       |
| created                             | 2016-01-31T16:34:15Z                                  |
| flavor                              | m1.tiny (1)                                           |
| hostId                              |                                                       |
| id                                  | 5b535f1e-1f6e-47f1-a527-3c4b56d38589                  |
| image                               | cirros-0.3.4-x86_64 (952c8431-f534-4c5f-bc06-c6122f112232) |
| key_name                            | -                                                     |
| metadata                            | {}                                                    |
| name                                | MyDirectInstance                                      |
| os-extended-volumes:volumes_attached | []                                                   |
| progress                            | 0                                                     |
| security_groups                     | default                                               |
| status                              | BUILD                                                 |
| tenant_id                           | c51a93428ada44f297e5fe65a3ac3b9f                      |
| updated                             | 2016-01-31T16:34:16Z                                  |
| user_id                             | f3596d7861514f92aae527ba6dec3e25                      |
+-------------------------------------+-------------------------------------------------------+
```

Use the `nova list` command to view a list of instances associated with your tenant or project. If you know the name or the ID of the instance, use the `nova show` command to provide additional details about the instance. Instances can also be viewed from the **Project | Compute | Instances** page in **Horizon** dashboard, as shown in the following screenshot:

Accessing the instance

Once the virtual machine instance has been created, navigate to the **Project | Compute | Instances** page and select **Console** from the **Actions** menu of the `MyDirectInstance` instance:

As long as the virtual machine is in the **Active** state, a virtual console will load within the browser window that will allow you to interface with the virtual machine:

```
                Connected (unencrypted) to: QEMU (instance-00000002)
evel@redhat.com
[    1.093949] cpuidle: using governor ladder
[    1.094046] cpuidle: using governor menu
[    1.094111] EFI Variables Facility v0.08 2004-May-17
[    1.099030] TCP cubic registered
[    1.101307] NET: Registered protocol family 10
[    1.110171] NET: Registered protocol family 17
[    1.110375] Registering the dns_resolver key type
[    1.110477] registered taskstats version 1
[    1.207576]    Magic number: 0:721:90
[    1.210429] rtc_cmos 00:01: setting system clock to 2016-01-31 18:04:14 UTC (
1454263454)
[    1.210624] powernow-k8: Processor cpuid 6d3 not supported
[    1.211346] BIOS EDD facility v0.16 2004-Jun-25, 0 devices found
[    1.211450] EDD information not available.
[    1.221463] Freeing unused kernel memory: 928k freed
[    1.231779] Write protecting the kernel read-only data: 12288k
[    1.265974] Freeing unused kernel memory: 1596k freed
[    1.279631] Freeing unused kernel memory: 1184k freed

further output written to /dev/ttyS0


login as 'cirros' user. default password: 'cubswin:)'. use 'sudo' for root.
cirros login: _
```

 Depending on the specifications of the client workstation hosting this environment, booting and using virtual machine instances within the virtual machine hosting the OpenStack environment may be a bit sluggish. If the console appears to be stalled, take a break and grab a cup of coffee!

Once the login prompt appears, authenticate using the following credentials:

- Username: cirros
- Password: cubswin:)

Using the `ip addr` and `ip route` commands, verify that the instance received its IP address and routes from the DHCP server created and managed by Neutron:

```
                 Connected (unencrypted) to: QEMU (instance-00000002)
$ whoami
cirros
$
$ ip a
1: lo: <LOOPBACK,UP,LOWER_UP> mtu 16436 qdisc noqueue
    link/loopback 00:00:00:00:00:00 brd 00:00:00:00:00:00
    inet 127.0.0.1/8 scope host lo
    inet6 ::1/128 scope host
       valid_lft forever preferred_lft forever
2: eth0: <BROADCAST,MULTICAST,UP,LOWER_UP> mtu 1400 qdisc pfifo_fast qlen 1000
    link/ether fa:16:3e:87:4e:0b brd ff:ff:ff:ff:ff:ff
    inet 10.50.0.3/24 brd 10.50.0.255 scope global eth0     .
    inet6 fe80::f816:3eff:fe87:4e0b/64 scope link
       valid_lft forever preferred_lft forever
$
$ ip r
default via 10.50.0.1 dev eth0
10.50.0.0/24 dev eth0  src 10.50.0.3
$
$ _
```

In this example, the instance was assigned the fixed IP 10.50.0.3 upon boot, and that's exactly what the Neutron DHCP server handed out to the instance. The default gateway is 10.50.0.1, an external gateway device not managed by Neutron or OpenStack.

 In this VirtualBox-based environment, 10.50.0.1 is an IP address automatically configured on the workstation hosting VirtualBox. For the sake of these exercises, just pretend it's a physical routing device.

From the console window, issue a `ping` to the gateway address to verify outbound connectivity from the instance to the gateway:

```
Connected (unencrypted) to: QEMU (instance-00000002)
$ ping 10.50.0.1 -c 5
PING 10.50.0.1 (10.50.0.1): 56 data bytes
64 bytes from 10.50.0.1: seq=0 ttl=64 time=0.921 ms
64 bytes from 10.50.0.1: seq=1 ttl=64 time=0.658 ms
64 bytes from 10.50.0.1: seq=2 ttl=64 time=0.558 ms
64 bytes from 10.50.0.1: seq=3 ttl=64 time=0.540 ms
64 bytes from 10.50.0.1: seq=4 ttl=64 time=0.573 ms

--- 10.50.0.1 ping statistics ---
5 packets transmitted, 5 packets received, 0% packet loss
round-trip min/avg/max = 0.540/0.650/0.921 ms
$ _
```

A response from the gateway indicates that Neutron has properly configured the network plumbing on our host based on the network driver in use. In this environment, using Open vSwitch, Nova has attached the instance to the integration bridge and Neutron has created OpenFlow rules that help bridge the virtual network to the physical network. Neutron has also created security rules on the node to allow outbound access, which will be looked at in further detail in *Chapter 8, Security Group Fundamentals*.

Because the instance is connected directly to the provider network, our client workstation should be able to connect to the instance directly via its fixed IP, thanks in part to a security group rule allowing SSH access that we added back in *Chapter 2, Installing OpenStack Using RDO*. Using an SSH client, connect to the instance and authenticate using the following credentials:

- Username: `cirros`
- Password: `cubswin:)`

The following screenshot demonstrates a connection from my local workstation to the fixed IP of the virtual machine instance:

```
retina-imac:~ jdenton$ ssh cirros@10.50.0.3
The authenticity of host '10.50.0.3 (10.50.0.3)' can't be established.
RSA key fingerprint is SHA256:xvpZI+nz/K1tSqU2dChNSeEdWOVtQpIK7Naa9o/MKxY.
Are you sure you want to continue connecting (yes/no)? yes
Warning: Permanently added '10.50.0.3' (RSA) to the list of known hosts.
cirros@10.50.0.3's password:
$ exit
Connection to 10.50.0.3 closed.
```

 In a real environment, provider networks should be routable within the corporate network. In this test environment, the client workstation has an interface in the provider network by way of the VirtualBox network configuration.

Using a Neutron router

If you recall from *Chapter 3, Neutron API Basics*, users can create and manage networks known as tenant networks that are completely isolated from other networks and tenants via **Layer 2** segregation. Users do not require any knowledge of the physical infrastructure when creating tenant networks and are not aware of the underlying **Layer 2** technology that provides connectivity between hosts, be it VLAN, VXLAN, GRE, or some other technology.

Users can use Neutron routers to provide flexibility in networking by connecting user-created tenant networks to one another and to the physical network. Neutron routers act as NAT gateways in an effort to provide connectivity to and from virtual machine instances in tenant networks. In the following diagram, a Neutron router is connected to both a provider network and a user-created tenant network:

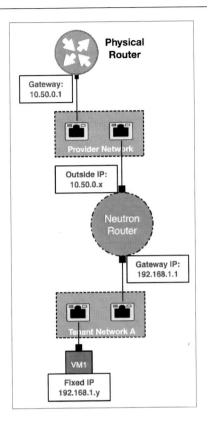

When instances are placed behind a Neutron router, users can no longer access them directly by their fixed IP. Instead, users must create **Network Address Translations (NATs)** using floating IPs or utilize virtual private networks by way of **VPN as a Service (VPNaaS)**.

> Future releases of OpenStack Neutron will support the use of BGP to advertise tenant network address space rather than relying completely on NAT. In some advanced configurations, tenant networks may be routed from upstream routers to Neutron routers using static routes. For this configuration to work, SNAT must be disabled on the Neutron router using the `--disable-snat` flag with the `router-gateway-set` command. This is not a common configuration, but it has to be mentioned nonetheless.

External provider networks

Neutron routers look and act much like traditional routers in that they have what can be considered a **Wide Area Network (WAN)** interface known as a **gateway interface** and one or more **Local Area Network (LAN)** interfaces known as **internal** or **router interfaces**. In Neutron-speak, the WAN (or gateway) interface connects to a provider network and the LAN (or router) interfaces connect to tenant networks.

So far, we've learned that instances connected to tenant networks behind a Neutron router are not directly accessible without the use of a floating IP or NAT. External provider networks are unique in that they act as the floating IP pool for attached routers. What makes a provider network an external provider network, you ask? Why, the `external` attribute provided by the `external-net` extension, that's what!

In the previous section, we created a provider network and attached instances directly to it. Before a router can be attached to a provider network, however, the network's `external` attribute must be set to `True`. A Neutron router must be connected to an external provider network to provide a path for traffic into, or out of, connected tenant networks.

 Only a user with the `admin` role can set the `external` attribute of a network.

Using the `neutron net-update` command, update the provider network accordingly:

```
[root@allinone ~(keystone_admin)]# neutron net-update MyExternalProviderNetwork --router:external=true
Updated network: MyExternalProviderNetwork

[root@allinone ~(keystone_admin)]# neutron net-show MyExternalProviderNetwork
+---------------------------+--------------------------------------+
| Field                     | Value                                |
+---------------------------+--------------------------------------+
| admin_state_up            | True                                 |
| id                        | 52550637-519f-496d-afd1-75ab7ff51e44 |
| mtu                       | 0                                    |
| name                      | MyExternalProviderNetwork            |
| provider:network_type     | flat                                 |
| provider:physical_network | physnet1                             |
| provider:segmentation_id  |                                      |
| router:external           | True                                 |
| shared                    | False                                |
| status                    | ACTIVE                               |
| subnets                   | fe581964-41b0-42c6-b08e-b09ca254d631 |
| tenant_id                 | c51a93428ada44f297e5fe65a3ac3b9f     |
+---------------------------+--------------------------------------+
```

Attaching the router to an external provider network

There are two Neutron CLI commands used to attach Neutron routers to networks. They are:

- `router-gateway-set`: This connects a Neutron router to a provider network
- `router-interface-add`: This connects a Neutron router to a tenant network

The `router-gateway-set` command requires two pieces of information: the router name or ID and the external provider network name or ID. Once it is issued, Neutron creates a port and allocates an IP address to the router's external interface from the allocation pool of the network's subnet. The Neutron L3 agent then configures the interface inside the network namespace and sets the `default` gateway to that specified by the respective subnet.

Within **Horizon** dashboard, Neutron routers can be connected to provider networks from the **Project** | **Network** | **Routers** page, seen here:

To set a gateway, perform the following steps:

1. Click on the **Set Gateway** button from the **Actions** menu next to the router. Doing so will bring up the **Set Gateway** wizard, seen here:

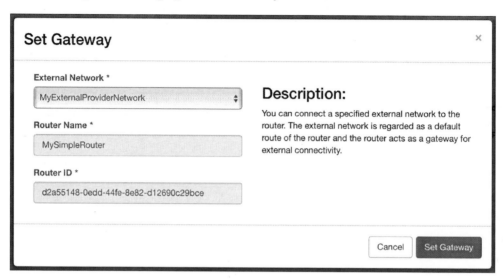

2. Choose a provider network from the list; this will serve as the external network for the router.

 Only provider networks whose `external` attribute is set to `true` will appear in the list, so don't worry if you don't see any other networks. In addition, external provider networks are visible to all tenants, regardless of whether or not the `shared` attribute is set.

3. Click on the blue **Set Gateway** button to complete the wizard and return to the **Routers** page. The external network will be listed next to the router:

4. To clear the gateway, click on the red **Clear Gateway** button.

Neutron will not allow you to clear the gateway of a router if floating IPs have been assigned to instances behind the router. The floating IPs must be unallocated first before the gateway can be cleared.

Booting an instance

Using the `nova boot` command or the **Horizon** dashboard, boot an instance and connect it to the `MySimpleNetwork` network created in the previous chapter. To boot the instance in **Horizon** dashboard, complete the following steps:

1. From the **Project | Compute | Instances** page, click on the **Add Instance** button to launch the wizard:

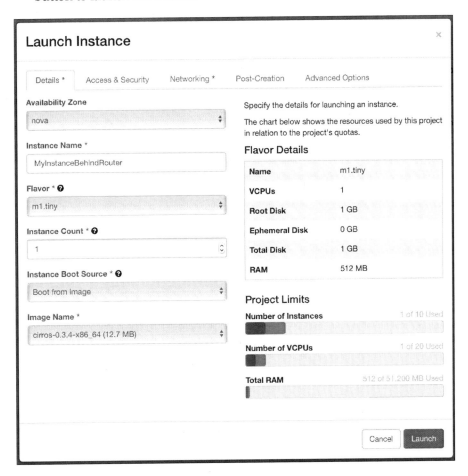

2. Name the instance, choose the image and flavor, and hit the **Access & Security** tab to continue.

3. From the **Access & Security** tab, choose the **default** security group and click on the **Networking** tab to continue:

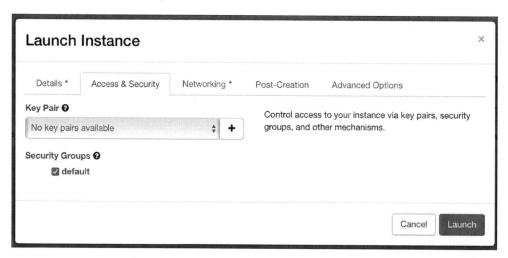

4. From the **Networking** tab, move the MySimpleNetwork network to the **Selected networks** box using the blue plus (+) sign:

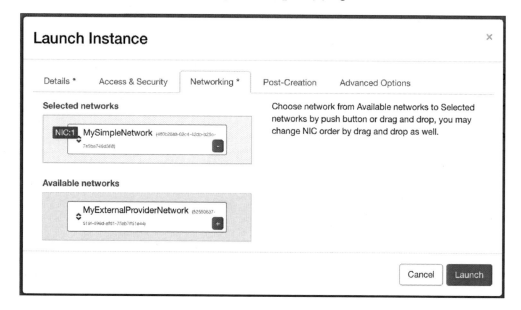

5. Click on the blue **Launch** button to complete the wizard. The instance should begin the boot process and will be reflected in the instance list:

Testing connectivity

So far, we have built a network that resembles the following logical diagram:

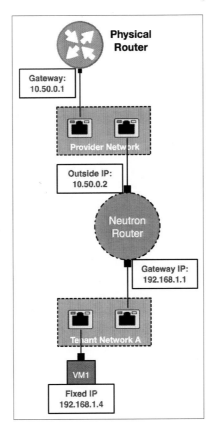

In the logical diagram, the Neutron router, known as `MySimpleRouter`, serves as the gateway for the virtual machine instance known as `MyInstanceBehindRouter`. The physical router, in turn, serves as the gateway for the Neutron router.

Unlike the `MyDirectInstance` virtual machine created earlier in this chapter, the virtual machine known as `MyInstanceBehindRouter` cannot be reached directly via its fixed IP. Any attempt to connect to the virtual machine from the client workstation via its fixed IP address in this configuration will be unsuccessful:

```
retina-imac:~ jdenton$ ssh cirros@192.168.1.4
ssh: connect to host 192.168.1.4 port 22: Operation timed out
```

At this point, the only way to manage the instance is through the console in **Horizon**. To access the instance, perform the following steps:

1. From the **Project | Compute | Instances** page, select **Console** from the **Actions** menu of the `MyInstanceBehindRouter` instance to open a virtual console:

```
Connected (unencrypted) to: QEMU (instance-00000003)
[    0.746236] cpuidle: using governor ladder
[    0.746333] cpuidle: using governor menu
[    0.746397] EFI Variables Facility v0.08 2004-May-17
[    0.749310] TCP cubic registered
[    0.750032] NET: Registered protocol family 10
[    0.756590] NET: Registered protocol family 17
[    0.756843] Registering the dns_resolver key type
[    0.759753] registered taskstats version 1
[    0.844324]   Magic number: 0:718:189
[    0.844582] acpi device:1b: hash matches
[    0.844937] rtc_cmos 00:01: setting system clock to 2016-01-31 17:11:49 UTC (
1454260309)
[    0.845103] powernow-k8: Processor cpuid 6d3 not supported
[    0.845770] BIOS EDD facility v0.16 2004-Jun-25, 0 devices found
[    0.845862] EDD information not available.
[    0.872258] Freeing unused kernel memory: 928k freed
[    0.883933] Write protecting the kernel read-only data: 12288k
[    0.905902] Freeing unused kernel memory: 1596k freed
[    0.920286] Freeing unused kernel memory: 1184k freed

further output written to /dev/ttyS0


login as 'cirros' user. default password: 'cubswin:)'. use 'sudo' for root.
myinstancebehindrouter login:
```

2. Once the login prompt appears, authenticate using the following credentials:

   ○   Username: `cirros`

   ○   Password: `cubswin:)`

3. Using the `ip addr` and `ip route` commands, verify that the instance received its IP address and routes from the DHCP server created and managed by Neutron:

```
                    Connected (unencrypted) to: QEMU (instance-00000003)

further output written to /dev/ttyS0


login as 'cirros' user, default password: 'cubswin:)'. use 'sudo' for root.
myinstancebehindrouter login: cirros
Password:
$ whoami
cirros
$ ip a
1: lo: <LOOPBACK,UP,LOWER_UP> mtu 16436 qdisc noqueue
    link/loopback 00:00:00:00:00:00 brd 00:00:00:00:00:00
    inet 127.0.0.1/8 scope host lo
    inet6 ::1/128 scope host
       valid_lft forever preferred_lft forever
2: eth0: <BROADCAST,MULTICAST,UP,LOWER_UP> mtu 1400 qdisc pfifo_fast qlen 1000
    link/ether fa:16:3e:1c:14:15 brd ff:ff:ff:ff:ff:ff
    inet 192.168.1.4/24 brd 192.168.1.255 scope global eth0
    inet6 fe80::f816:3eff:fe1c:1415/64 scope link
       valid_lft forever preferred_lft forever
$ ip r
default via 192.168.1.1 dev eth0
169.254.169.254 via 192.168.1.1 dev eth0
192.168.1.0/24 dev eth0  src 192.168.1.4
$ _
```

In this example, the instance was assigned the fixed IP 192.168.1.4 upon boot, and the eth0 interface has been configured accordingly using DHCP. The default route directs traffic to 192.168.1.1, an address owned by and configured on the Neutron router. To test routing capabilities through the Neutron router, issue a ping to the external gateway device at 10.50.0.1:

```
Connected (unencrypted) to: QEMU (instance-00000003)
$ ping 10.50.0.1
PING 10.50.0.1 (10.50.0.1): 56 data bytes
64 bytes from 10.50.0.1: seq=0 ttl=63 time=1.395 ms
64 bytes from 10.50.0.1: seq=1 ttl=63 time=0.787 ms
64 bytes from 10.50.0.1: seq=2 ttl=63 time=0.569 ms
64 bytes from 10.50.0.1: seq=3 ttl=63 time=0.608 ms
64 bytes from 10.50.0.1: seq=4 ttl=63 time=0.583 ms

--- 10.50.0.1 ping statistics ---
5 packets transmitted, 5 packets received, 0% packet loss
round-trip min/avg/max = 0.569/0.788/1.395 ms
$ _
```

In this VirtualBox-based environment, 10.50.0.1 is an IP address automatically configured on the workstation hosting VirtualBox. For the sake of these exercises, we'll just pretend it's a physical router.

In this example, the ping from the virtual machine instance has been routed through the Neutron router to the external gateway device at 10.50.0.1. A response from 10.50.0.1 indicates that Neutron has properly configured the virtual switches and the virtual router. In this environment, using Open vSwitch, Nova attached the instance to the integration bridge and Neutron created OpenFlow rules that helped bridge the virtual network to the physical network. In addition, Neutron configured the virtual router with a source NAT rule to ensure return traffic can make it back to our instance. We'll take a look at this in the next section.

Observing SNAT behavior

Using `tcpdump` on our external gateway device (a.k.a. the client workstation), we can confirm that the `ping` from the instance was received and responded to:

```
retina-imac:~ jdenton$ sudo tcpdump -i any host 10.50.0.1 and icmp
Password:
tcpdump: data link type PKTAP
tcpdump: verbose output suppressed, use -v or -vv for full protocol decode
listening on any, link-type PKTAP (Packet Tap), capture size 262144 bytes
11:12:42.218610 IP 10.50.0.2 > 10.50.0.1: ICMP echo request, id 12033, seq 0, length 64
11:12:42.218641 IP 10.50.0.1 > 10.50.0.2: ICMP echo reply, id 12033, seq 0, length 64
11:12:43.219151 IP 10.50.0.2 > 10.50.0.1: ICMP echo request, id 12033, seq 1, length 64
11:12:43.219180 IP 10.50.0.1 > 10.50.0.2: ICMP echo reply, id 12033, seq 1, length 64
11:12:44.219544 IP 10.50.0.2 > 10.50.0.1: ICMP echo request, id 12033, seq 2, length 64
11:12:44.219566 IP 10.50.0.1 > 10.50.0.2: ICMP echo reply, id 12033, seq 2, length 64
11:12:45.219875 IP 10.50.0.2 > 10.50.0.1: ICMP echo request, id 12033, seq 3, length 64
11:12:45.219905 IP 10.50.0.1 > 10.50.0.2: ICMP echo reply, id 12033, seq 3, length 64
11:12:46.220583 IP 10.50.0.2 > 10.50.0.1: ICMP echo request, id 12033, seq 4, length 64
11:12:46.220612 IP 10.50.0.1 > 10.50.0.2: ICMP echo reply, id 12033, seq 4, length 64
```

Rather than coming from the instance's fixed IP address, however, the source of the `ping` appears to be `10.50.0.2`. If you recall from *Chapter 6, Routing*, the source address of all outbound traffic from instances behind a Neutron router without floating IPs is modified to use the router's external address. To determine the external address of a router, use the `neutron router-show` command. The external address can be found in the `external_gateway_info` field, seen here:

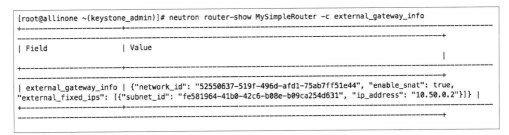

```
[root@allinone ~(keystone_admin)]# neutron router-show MySimpleRouter -c external_gateway_info
+----------------------+--------------------------------------------------------------------+
| Field                | Value                                                              |
+----------------------+--------------------------------------------------------------------+
| external_gateway_info | {"network_id": "52550637-519f-496d-afd1-75ab7ff51e44", "enable_snat": true,
"external_fixed_ips": [{"subnet_id": "fe581964-41b0-42c6-b08e-b09ca254d631", "ip_address": "10.50.0.2"}]} |
+----------------------+--------------------------------------------------------------------+
```

The use of source NAT to dynamically allow outbound access is extremely handy, but it is not at all useful for connecting inbound traffic to instances. For that to happen, we'll need a 1:1 network address translation, known as a **floating IP**.

Assigning a floating IP

If you recall from the previous chapter, a floating IP is an address that is used to provide a 1:1 static NAT to a single fixed IP. Floating IPs provide clients the ability to reach individual virtual machine instances and other devices that are attached to networks behind Neutron routers using a unique, routable address.

There are four Neutron CLI commands used to manage floating IPs. They are:

- `floatingip-create`: This creates a floating IP
- `floatingip-associate`: This associates a floating IP with a Neutron port
- `floatingip-disassociate`: This disassociates a floating IP from a Neutron port
- `floatingip-delete`: This deletes a floating IP

The `floatingip-create` command requires the external network name or ID to procure the address from. The `floatingip-associate` command requires the ID of both the floating IP and the Neutron port. Once it is issued, Neutron automatically determines the router to apply the NAT rule to. The Neutron L3 agent will configure the NAT using iptables inside the respective router network namespace.

Within **Horizon**, floating IPs can be associated with instances from the **Project | Compute | Instance** page, seen here:

To create and assign a floating IP, perform the following steps:

1. Click on the **Associate Floating IP** button from the **Actions** menu next to the instance to bring up the **Manage Floating IP Associations** wizard, seen here:

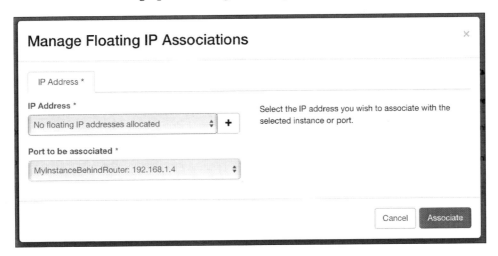

2. Existing floating IP allocations are listed in the **IP Address** menu. Select an available address from the **IP Address** menu or, if none are available, click on the plus (**+**) sign to create a new floating IP. The **Allocate Floating IP** wizard will appear:

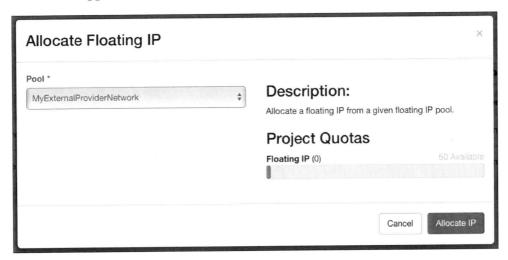

3. Choose the pool from which the floating IP address will be sourced. The only eligible network is the external network attached to the Neutron router. Click on the blue **Allocate IP** button to allocate a new floating IP and return to the previous wizard:

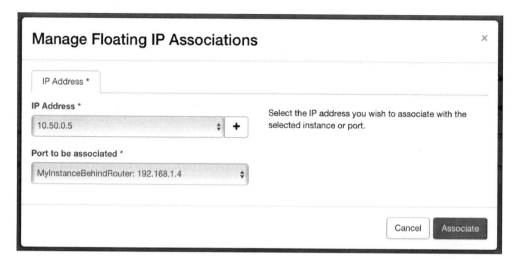

4. The newly allocated floating IP address should appear in the **IP Addresses** menu. Click on the blue **Associate** button to associate the floating IP with the port listed in the **Port to be associated** menu and return to the **Instances** page:

Testing connectivity via floating IP

Now that a floating IP has been associated with the instance, connecting to the instance should be quick and easy, provided the appropriate access is permitted. From the client workstation, SSH to the floating IP address assigned in the previous section:

```
retina-imac:~ jdenton$ ssh cirros@10.50.0.5
The authenticity of host '10.50.0.5 (10.50.0.5)' can't be established.
RSA key fingerprint is SHA256:vkHKLrnBdy29h8vtOZGPo5XvK3bvU2c9uRyNoRyJ4x8.
Are you sure you want to continue connecting (yes/no)? yes
Warning: Permanently added '10.50.0.5' (RSA) to the list of known hosts.
cirros@10.50.0.5's password:
$ ip a
1: lo: <LOOPBACK,UP,LOWER_UP> mtu 16436 qdisc noqueue
    link/loopback 00:00:00:00:00:00 brd 00:00:00:00:00:00
    inet 127.0.0.1/8 scope host lo
    inet6 ::1/128 scope host
       valid_lft forever preferred_lft forever
2: eth0: <BROADCAST,MULTICAST,UP,LOWER_UP> mtu 1400 qdisc pfifo_fast qlen 1000
    link/ether fa:16:3e:1c:14:15 brd ff:ff:ff:ff:ff:ff
    inet 192.168.1.4/24 brd 192.168.1.255 scope global eth0
    inet6 fe80::f816:3eff:fe1c:1415/64 scope link
       valid_lft forever preferred_lft forever
```

A quick look at the interfaces within the instance shows the fixed IP configured on eth0. Given that we were able to SSH to the instance from the client workstation, pinging the external gateway address at 10.50.0.1 should prove successful as well:

```
$ ping 10.50.0.1 -c 5
PING 10.50.0.1 (10.50.0.1): 56 data bytes
64 bytes from 10.50.0.1: seq=0 ttl=63 time=1.144 ms
64 bytes from 10.50.0.1: seq=1 ttl=63 time=0.685 ms
64 bytes from 10.50.0.1: seq=2 ttl=63 time=0.657 ms
64 bytes from 10.50.0.1: seq=3 ttl=63 time=0.616 ms
64 bytes from 10.50.0.1: seq=4 ttl=63 time=0.655 ms

--- 10.50.0.1 ping statistics ---
5 packets transmitted, 5 packets received, 0% packet loss
round-trip min/avg/max = 0.616/0.751/1.144 ms
```

Another packet capture on the external gateway device (a.k.a. the client workstation) reflects the source of the ping as the floating IP address, proving that the Neutron router is performing the 1:1 NAT as expected:

```
retina-imac:~ jdenton$ sudo tcpdump -i any host 10.50.0.1 and icmp
Password:
tcpdump: data link type PKTAP
tcpdump: verbose output suppressed, use -v or -vv for full protocol decode
listening on any, link-type PKTAP (Packet Tap), capture size 262144 bytes
11:15:48.799275 IP 10.50.0.5 > 10.50.0.1: ICMP echo request, id 14081, seq 0, length 64
11:15:48.799286 IP 10.50.0.1 > 10.50.0.5: ICMP echo reply, id 14081, seq 0, length 64
11:15:49.799741 IP 10.50.0.5 > 10.50.0.1: ICMP echo request, id 14081, seq 1, length 64
11:15:49.799771 IP 10.50.0.1 > 10.50.0.5: ICMP echo reply, id 14081, seq 1, length 64
11:15:50.800333 IP 10.50.0.5 > 10.50.0.1: ICMP echo request, id 14081, seq 2, length 64
11:15:50.800366 IP 10.50.0.1 > 10.50.0.5: ICMP echo reply, id 14081, seq 2, length 64
11:15:51.800756 IP 10.50.0.5 > 10.50.0.1: ICMP echo request, id 14081, seq 3, length 64
11:15:51.800789 IP 10.50.0.1 > 10.50.0.5: ICMP echo reply, id 14081, seq 3, length 64
11:15:52.801375 IP 10.50.0.5 > 10.50.0.1: ICMP echo request, id 14081, seq 4, length 64
11:15:52.801403 IP 10.50.0.1 > 10.50.0.5: ICMP echo reply, id 14081, seq 4, length 64
```

 Floating IP addresses can only be associated with a single port and fixed IP at a time, meaning that identifying traffic on upstream devices from naughty virtual machine instances is much simpler than the SNAT scenario.

Multiple routers

Multiple routers can be attached to the same provider network in a logical configuration similar to the one pictured here:

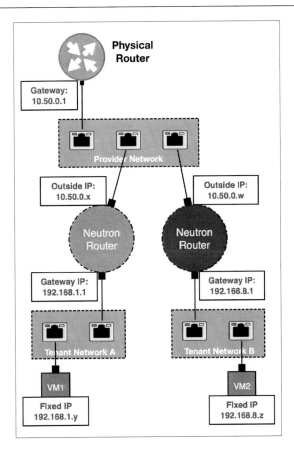

Communication between instances behind different Neutron routers must be done using floating IPs, since the tenant networks themselves are not routable outside of their respective routers.

Advanced networking

Virtual machine instances can be multi-homed, meaning they can have more than one network interface that connects to different networks. A combination of admin-defined provider networks and user-defined tenant networks can be used to build advanced network architectures. Using multiple network interfaces on the physical nodes, provider networks can be created that leverage different switching infrastructures with capabilities that range from 1/10/40 Gigabit Ethernet to InfiniBand and more. If you specify multiple provider bridge mappings in the Neutron configuration file and create the respective networks using the API, the sky really is the limit.

Looking ahead to future releases, users connecting to instances behind Neutron routers won't be limited to using floating IPs. Instead, users will be able to leverage BGP configured in Neutron routers to automatically announce routes to tenant networks to upstream routers, simplifying connectivity to those instances across the network.

For more information on the future use of BGP and address scopes with Neutron routers, check out the following resources:

https://www.openstack.org/summit/tokyo-2015/videos/presentation/neutron-and-bgp-dynamic-routing.

https://www.youtube.com/watch?v=QqP8yBUUXBM&t=6m12s.

http://docs.openstack.org/developer/neutron/devref/address_scopes.html.

Summary

In this chapter, we looked at some basic network architectures found in many OpenStack clouds that utilize Neutron networking. For performance and simplicity in operations and troubleshooting, many users find connecting instances directly to provider networks the best option when available. For users who want to have a hand in the overall network architecture in order to meet complex network requirements, using tenant networks and Neutron routers provides features and functionality above and beyond what provider networks alone can do. Not to mention, Neutron routers are a requirement for advanced Neutron services, such as **Firewall as a Service**, **Load Balancer as a Service**, and **VPN as a Service** in a reference implementation. When building a network architecture to support your application, try drawing a logical diagram similar to the ones pictured in this chapter to get a good idea of traffic flow between networks and instances before implementing the networks in Neutron.

In the next chapter, we will look at securing traffic between instances and external networks using Neutron security groups. While drawing the traffic flow, keep in mind security requirements, including access to ports and protocols, as we work through a few exercises in the next chapter.

8
Security Group Fundamentals

So far, we've looked at some common basic network architectures and even managed to build some virtual networks and routers of our own along the way. But what about security? You'll be happy to know that Neutron does its best to protect you from yourself and other users out of the box, but like many things, some tweaking and coordination may be involved in order to provide a strong security posture for instances and the applications hosted within them.

Neutron includes two methods of providing network-level security to instances: security groups and virtual firewalls. Security group functionality predates Neutron and provides traffic filtering at the individual virtual network interface level on compute nodes using iptables. Virtual firewalls, on the other hand, are provided by the advanced Neutron service known as **Firewall as a Service (FWaaS)**, which relies on iptables to filter traffic at the perimeter of the network within a Neutron router. In either case, it is important to know that Neutron is not responsible for implementing security rules on the instances themselves.

In this chapter, we will focus on securing network traffic to instances by covering such topics as:

- Security group fundamentals
- Default security group behavior
- Creating and managing security groups in the **CLI** and **Horizon** dashboard
- Disabling port security

Security groups in OpenStack

Think back to *Chapter 3, Neutron API Basics,* where we looked at the logical Neutron data model that consists of networks, subnets, and ports. Every logical Neutron port related to a virtual machine instance equates to a virtual network interface on a compute node that gets connected to a virtual switch, similar to what is pictured here:

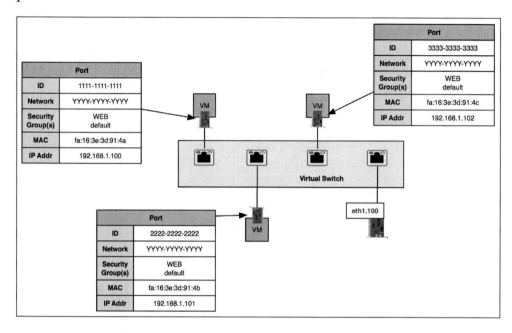

In traditional environments, users rely on traffic filtering performed at the edge of the network on a physical firewall device or within the guest operating system using a software-based firewall such as iptables or Windows Firewall. In an OpenStack-based cloud, Neutron provides an API for applying OS-agnostic traffic filters at each port as it connects to the virtual switch rather than applying them within the guest OS, or anywhere else for that matter, using what are called **security groups**. A security group is a collection of network access rules known as security group rules applied to Neutron ports, and these limit the types of traffic an instance or, more specifically, a particular network interface can send or receive.

The basics characteristics of Neutron security groups are as follows:

- Security groups are tenant or project-owned objects and cannot be shared or referenced across projects
- For ingress traffic (traffic *to* an instance):
    - Only traffic that matches a security group rule is allowed
    - All other inbound traffic that does not match a rule is dropped

- For egress traffic (traffic *from* an instance)
    - Only traffic that matches a security group rule is allowed
    - All other outbound traffic that does not match a rule is dropped

- Security groups require port security to be enabled on a particular port
- Newly-created security groups include rules that allow all egress traffic and no ingress traffic
- Security group rules can reference other security groups rather than IP addresses or networks
- Each project has a default security group that gets applied to every port by default:
    - The default security group allows all egress traffic and includes an ingress rule that references the default group
    - As a result, intercommunication between instances in the default group is allowed

Using security groups

There are multiple ways in which security groups can be used. For example, one or more instances, usually of similar functionality or role, can be placed in a security group. Security group rules can reference IPv4 and IPv6 hosts and networks as well as security groups themselves. Referencing a particular security group in a rule, rather than a particular host or network, frees the user from having to specify individual addresses. Neutron will automatically construct the filtering rules applied on the host, based on network information in the Neutron database.

Security group management can get a bit unruly, especially for a port associated with multiple security groups. A simple example of ports each belonging to a single security group can be seen in the following diagram:

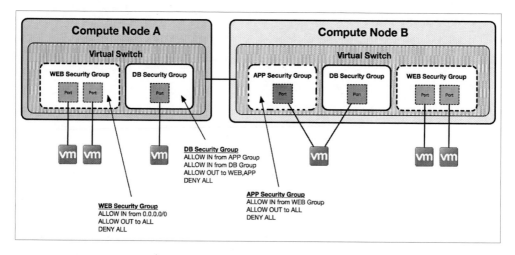

In the diagram, ports connected to the virtual switch belong to one of three security groups: **WEB**, **DB**, or **APP**. When a change is made to a security group, such as adding or removing group rules, corresponding filter rule changes are made automatically on the compute nodes for every port associated with the security group.

Another way security groups get used is for describing certain types of rules that should be applied to a particular instance port. For example, a security group can be used to categorize multiple hosts or subnets that are allowed access to a port. Multiple security groups can be applied to a port, and all rules defined in those groups are applied to the port.

 Remember, all traffic though a port is implicitly denied. Security group rules can only define the traffic that should be allowed through a port. Because of this, there is no chance of a rule in one security group applied to a port counteracting or overriding a rule in another security group applied to the same port. There is no order in which the rules should be applied since they are all ALLOW rules.

The following example demonstrates the use of security groups to categorize traffic that is allowed access through a port:

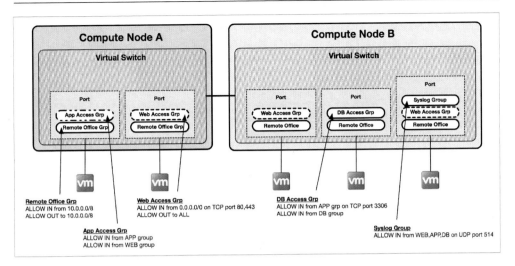

When a port is created in Neutron, it is associated with a default security group unless a specific one is specified. The default security group drops all ingress traffic and allows all egress traffic from instances. Rules can be added to or removed from the default security group to change its behavior. In addition, standard rules are applied to every instance that prohibit IP, DHCP, and MAC address spoofing. This behavior can be changed and will be discussed later in this chapter.

The default security group

The default security group that is created automatically by Neutron for each project contains four rules:

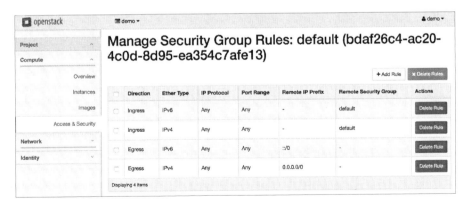

- **Ingress | IPv6 | Any | default**: This is a rule that states that any port associated with the default group is an allowed source of traffic

- **Ingress | IPv4 | Any | default**: This is a rule that states that any port associated with the default group is an allowed source of traffic

- **Egress | IPv6 | Any**: This is a rule that allows all outbound traffic to any remote IPv6 address

- **Egress | IPv4 | Any**: This is a rule that allows all outbound traffic to any remote IPv4 address

Subsequent security groups created within a project will only contain the two egress rules.

Back in *Chapter 2, Installing OpenStack Using RDO*, we created a security group rule that allowed SSH access to instances over TCP port 22 and applied it to the default security group in the admin project, as shown here:

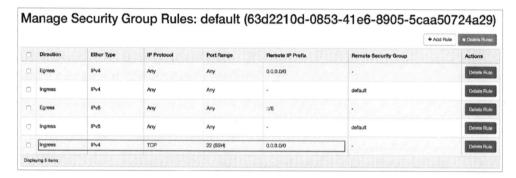

The result is that clients from any location can access **SSH** services on every instance spun up in the admin project, unless a user specifies otherwise by removing the default security group and applying another. As you build out security groups and associate rules, keep in mind some of the workflows and caveats described later in this chapter to maintain a proper security posture in your environment.

Managing security groups

Security groups can be managed using the Neutron CLI or the **Horizon** dashboard. From within the Neutron command-line client, a number of commands can be used to manage security groups, including:

- `security-group-create`
- `security-group-delete`
- `security-group-list`

- `security-group-rule-create`
- `security-group-rule-delete`
- `security-group-rule-list`
- `security-group-rule-show`
- `security-group-show`
- `security-group-update`

From the **Horizon** dashboard, security groups and rules are managed from the **Compute | Access & Security** panel.

Using CIDR to control traffic

Understanding how to properly subnet networks using the **Classless Inter-Domain Routing (CIDR)** notation is important for controlling access to instances. Using the wrong CIDR notation in a security group rule can expose your application and your environment to the Bad Guys™, a situation we'd like to prevent.

The following are some examples of networks using CIDR notation:

- `0.0.0.0/0` – This would allow traffic from all IP addresses
- `192.0.2.0/0` – This would still allow traffic from all IP addresses
- `192.0.2.0/8` – This would restrict traffic to IP addresses starting with `192.x.x.x`
- `192.0.2.0/16` – This would restrict traffic to IP addresses starting with `192.0.x.x`
- `192.0.2.0/24` – This would restrict traffic to IP addresses starting with `192.0.2.x`
- `192.0.2.1/32` – This would restrict traffic to a single host with IP address `192.0.2.1`

In many cases, instances exposed to the Internet will require looser security group rules to allow traffic from all over the world compared to instances that serve backend functions and don't require access to anything other than other groups or networks in the cloud. Limiting access to instances using security groups and other hardening techniques is a highly recommended security practice in either case.

Applying security groups to instances and ports

Security groups can be applied to instances using the Nova CLI, Neutron CLI, or Horizon dashboard. Many users find themselves applying security groups to instances at instance creation using the `nova boot` command, like this:

```
nova boot … --security-group <SECURITY_GROUP_ID> INSTANCE_NAME
```

Applying multiple security groups to an instance can be accomplished using a comma-separated list, as shown here:

```
nova boot … --security-group <SG_1>,<SG_2>,<SG_3> INSTANCE_NAME
```

When a security group is not specified, the `default` group that corresponds to the project or tenant creating the instance is used. Security groups can also be applied to running instances by using either the `neutron port-update` command or the `nova add-secgroup` command. The following example demonstrates the use of `port-update` to apply security groups to a port:

```
neutron port-update <PORT_ID> --security-group <SECURITY_GROUP_ID>
```

 Using `port-update` to assign security groups to a port will overwrite existing security group associations.

Multiple security groups can be associated with a Neutron port simultaneously. To apply multiple security groups to a port, use the `--security-group` flag before each security group:

```
neutron port-update <PORT_ID> \
--security-group <SECURITY_GROUP_ID1> \
--security-group <SECURITY_GROUP_ID2> \
--security-group <SECURITY_GROUP_ID3>
```

The following example demonstrates the use of the `nova add-secgroup` command to apply a security group to all ports connected to an instance:

```
nova add-secgroup <INSTANCE_ID> <SECURITY_GROUP_ID>
```

The `add-secgroup` command should be run once for each security group rule being added.

To remove security group rules from a port, use the `neutron port-update` command with the `--no-security-group` flag, as shown here:

```
neutron port-update <PORT_ID> --no-security-group
```

Working with security groups in the dashboard

Within the **Horizon** dashboard, security groups are managed within the **Access & Security** section under the **Compute** tab, shown here:

Creating a security group

To create a **Security Group**, click on the **Create Security Group** button in the upper right-hand corner of the screen. A window will appear that will allow you to create a security group:

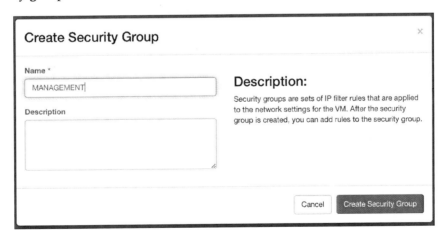

The **Name** field is required. When you are ready to proceed, click on the blue **Create Security Group** button to create the security group and return to the **Access & Security** page.

Managing security group rules

From the **Access & Security** page, you can add rules to a security group by clicking on the **Manage Rules** button of the corresponding group:

All the rules for the security group will be listed. By default, the security group will contain only egress rules. To add a rule, click on the **Add Rule** button in the upper right-hand corner, as shown here:

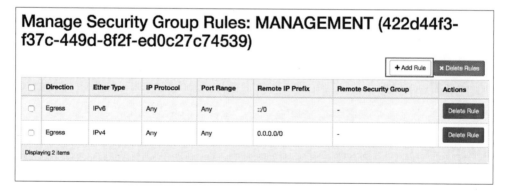

A window will appear that will allow you to create rules. Within the rule list, you can choose from a predefined list of protocols or create a custom rule. In the following example, we will create a rule that allows SSH access from networks matching the `10.0.0.0/8` CIDR, which includes our client workstation:

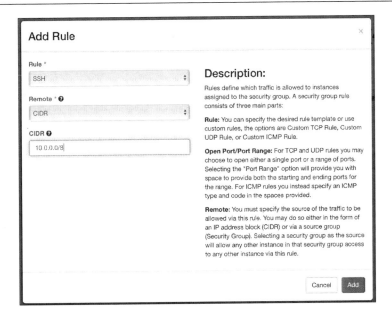

To complete the rule creation, click on the blue **Add** button.

Applying security groups to instances

To apply a security group to an instance, return to the **Instances** section of the **Compute** tab and perform the following steps:

1. Click on the arrow under the **Actions** menu next to the instance and choose **Edit Security Groups**:

2. A window will appear that allows you to apply or remove security groups from an instance. Remove any existing security group from the instance and apply the **MANAGEMENT** group only:

3. Click on the blue **Save** button to apply the changes and return to the **Instances** screen.

Caveats

Many workflows involve using the `nova boot` command or the **Horizon** dashboard to create instances with multiple network interfaces and security groups. When security groups are applied to an instance in the ways, there is no way of specifying which security group gets applied to a particular interface. The result is that all security groups passed to the command are applied to all of the interfaces. In most cases, this is an undesirable behavior.

When multi-homing an instance, it's best to adopt a workflow that involves creating Neutron ports first, applying the respective security groups to those ports, and then booting the instance with the `nova boot` command and specifying port IDs rather than network IDs, as shown here:

```
nova boot … --nic port-id=<PORT1> --nic port-id=<PORT2> <INSTANCE_NAME>
```

When using this method, it is important to remember to delete the ports after deleting the instance, as Nova will not automatically perform this function when attaching ports manually to instances. If you forget to delete the ports, expect to prematurely run out of IP addresses in the network!

Port security

In addition to providing users with a mechanism to allow inbound and outbound traffic to and from instances, Neutron also applies anti-spoofing rules to all ports to ensure that unexpected or undesired traffic cannot originate from, or pass through, a port. This includes rules that prohibit instances from acting as DHCP servers, acting as routers, or sourcing traffic from an IP address that is not its fixed IP. The latter is most often seen when setting up high availability between instances using **Virtual Router Redundancy Protocol** (**VRRP**), **keepalived**, or some other method. These security mechanisms are implemented by default for every port. However, there are two methods that can be used to work around or remove these security restrictions. They are:

- The `allowed-address-pairs` extension
- Disabling port security

Allowed address pairs

The `allowed-address-pairs` extension can be used to allow additional subnets and MAC addresses, other than the fixed IP and MAC address associated with the port, to act as source addresses for traffic leaving the port or virtual interface. This is useful when treating an instance as a routing device or VPN concentrator or when implementing high availability between multiple instances using addresses that need to "float" between them.

Existing allowed address pairs can be found in the details of each port using the `neutron port-show` command. For every network and/or MAC address that should be allowed, the `neutron port-update` command should be used with the `--allowed-address-pair` flag, as shown here:

```
neutron port-update <PORT_ID> \
--allowed-address-pairs type=dict list=true \
ip_address=<IP_ADDR>,mac_address=<MAC_ADDR>
```

The MAC address value is optional. If a MAC address is not specified, the MAC address of the port is used.

Multiple allowed address pairs can be associated with a Neutron port simultaneously. To apply multiple allowed address pairs to a port, simply specify multiple `ip_address` and `mac_address` key/value pairs, as shown here:

```
neutron port-update <PORT_ID> \
--allowed-address-pairs type=dict list=true \
ip_address=<IP_ADDR>,mac_address=<MAC_ADDR> \
ip_address=<IP_ADDR>,mac_address=<MAC_ADDR>
```

Using `port-update` to assign allowed address pairs to a port will overwrite existing address pairs.

Disabling port security

In Kilo, the `port security` extension was introduced for the ML2 plugin. It allows all packet filtering to be disabled on a port. Port security can be disabled at the individual port level or at the network level, which means that any port associated with a network will have port security disabled automatically. When port security is disabled, anti-spoofing rules are not applied. This is useful in cases such as **Network Functions Virtualization** (**NFV**), where an instance may serve as a virtual appliance that needs to perform network functions such as routing, firewalling, or more without being inhibited by standard port restrictions. On the flip side, disabling port security altogether means that instances can steal other instance IPs in the same network or act as rogue DHCP servers, resulting in issues that may take a while to troubleshoot and debug.

The `port security` extension requires additional configuration that will not be discussed in this book, and it is not enabled by default in this RDO installation.

When the `port security` extension is enabled, port security can be disabled on all ports connected to a particular network by setting the `port_security_enabled` attribute to `false` during network creation, like so:

```
[root@allinone jdenton(keystone_admin)]# neutron net-create TestNet-NoSecurity --port_security_enabled=false
Created a new network:
+---------------------------+--------------------------------------+
| Field                     | Value                                |
+---------------------------+--------------------------------------+
| admin_state_up            | True                                 |
| id                        | f83b53ff-7d62-40fb-8aae-b713dfa3986e |
| mtu                       | 0                                    |
| name                      | TestNet-NoSecurity                   |
| port_security_enabled     | False                                |
| provider:network_type     | vxlan                                |
| provider:physical_network |                                      |
| provider:segmentation_id  | 27                                   |
| router:external           | False                                |
| shared                    | False                                |
| status                    | ACTIVE                               |
| subnets                   |                                      |
| tenant_id                 | c51a93428ada44f297e5fe65a3ac3b9f     |
+---------------------------+--------------------------------------+
```

Port security can be disabled on an individual port by setting the `port_security_ enabled` attribute to `false` while creating or updating a port, as shown here:

```
[root@allinone jdenton(keystone_admin)]# neutron port-create --port-security-enabled=false MyDemoNetwork
Created a new port:
+-----------------------+-------------------------------------------------------------------------------------------------+
| Field                 | Value                                                                                           |
+-----------------------+-------------------------------------------------------------------------------------------------+
| admin_state_up        | True                                                                                            |
| allowed_address_pairs |                                                                                                 |
| binding:host_id       |                                                                                                 |
| binding:profile       | {}                                                                                              |
| binding:vif_details   | {}                                                                                              |
| binding:vif_type      | unbound                                                                                         |
| binding:vnic_type     | normal                                                                                          |
| device_id             |                                                                                                 |
| device_owner          |                                                                                                 |
| dns_assignment        | {"hostname": "host-192-168-8-3", "ip_address": "192.168.8.3", "fqdn": "host-192-168-8-3.openstacklocal."} |
| dns_name              |                                                                                                 |
| fixed_ips             | {"subnet_id": "6ee10d34-4d82-4901-9627-22a758096e52", "ip_address": "192.168.8.3"}              |
| id                    | 616e4a2c-6780-4f3d-abc6-6b8eb8e9a677                                                            |
| mac_address           | fa:16:3e:d2:5a:e7                                                                               |
| name                  |                                                                                                 |
| network_id            | c8cde907-9a30-4e86-8c31-11d11f56cb2c                                                            |
| port_security_enabled | False                                                                                           |
| security_groups       |                                                                                                 |
| status                | DOWN                                                                                            |
| tenant_id             | c51a93428ada44f297e5fe65a3ac3b9f                                                               |
+-----------------------+-------------------------------------------------------------------------------------------------+
```

Neutron does not allow `port security` to be disabled on a port associated with one or more security groups. Before disabling `port security`, be sure to remove all security groups from a port using the `port-update` command with the `--no-security-groups` flag. Disabling port security means that any filtering must be implemented within the guest operating system.

Summary

Security groups are fundamental for controlling access to instances by allowing users to create inbound and outbound rules that limit traffic to and from instances based on specific addresses, ports, protocols, and even other security groups. Default security groups are created by Neutron for every tenant or project, and these allow all outbound communication and restrict inbound communication to instances in the same default security group. Subsequent security groups are locked down even further, allowing only outbound communication and not allowing any inbound traffic at all unless modified by the user.

Security group rules are implemented on the compute nodes themselves and are triggered when traffic enters or leaves a virtual network interface belonging to an instance. Users are free to implement additional firewalls within the guest operating system, but they may find managing rules in both places a bit cumbersome. Many organizations still utilize and rely on physical firewall devices to provide additional filtering at the edge of the network, which may mean that coordination is required between users of the cloud and traditional security teams to ensure proper rules and actions are in place in all locations.

Networking is one of the most important components of OpenStack. In fact, I would argue that it is *the most important* component. After all, what good is a car without roads to take you where you need to go? In this book, we looked at core Neutron API objects consisting of networks, subnets, and ports, as well as all the essential features provided by OpenStack Networking, including switching, routing, and security. Development in OpenStack and, by extension, the Neutron project, moves very quickly, with a new release seen every 6 months. The core components and features of Neutron covered in this book should not be expected to change much in the near future, but extensions to the API are being added at a feverish pace and will provide welcome features and functionality. For up-to-date information on features, bugs, and other Neutron-related topics, be sure to subscribe to the OpenStack mailing lists at `http://lists.openstack.org`. You can also subscribe to bug notices on **LaunchPad** at `https://bugs.launchpad.net/neutron`. For more in-depth coverage of the topics found in this book, check out *Learning OpenStack Networking (Neutron), Second Edition*, available through Packt Publishing at `http://www.packtpub.com`.

Configuring VirtualBox

The examples provided in this book rely on an installation of OpenStack on a single virtual machine connected to three virtual networks built out in VirtualBox. This appendix is meant to assist with the setup of a virtual environment using VirtualBox so that many of the examples throughout the book can be followed. This appendix covers `VirtualBox 5.0.x` configuration on Mac OS X 10.11 (El Capitan).

Configuring VirtualBox networking

When configuring the OpenStack environment within VirtualBox, the following networks are required:

Network Type	Name	Network	Adapter Address	DHCP
NAT	<default>	<default>	<default>	Yes
Host-only	vboxnet0	10.254.254.0/24	10.254.254.1	No
Host-only	vboxnet1	10.50.0.0/24	10.50.0.1	No

The host-only networks will be configured within the **Preferences** window of the VirtualBox application, while the NAT network is a default network provided by VirtualBox that uses the host machine to provide outbound connectivity through the use of **Network Address Translation** (**NAT**). The configuration of the host-only networks is covered in the following sections.

Configuring host-only networks

To configure host-only networks within VirtualBox, open up the **Preferences** window. On a Mac OS X machine, this can be found under the **VirtualBox** menu. On a Windows machine, this can be found under the **File** menu. By default, the **General** settings window will appear:

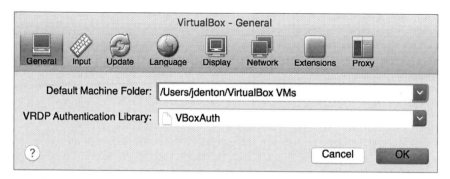

1. Click on the **Host-only Networks** button to reveal existing host-only networks:

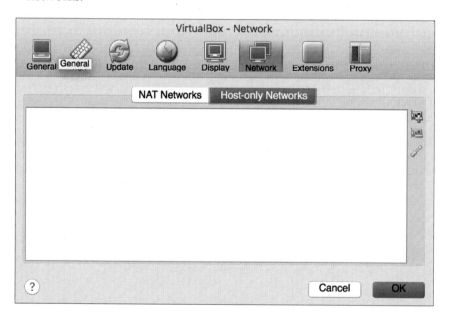

2. There are no **Host-only Networks** defined by default. On the right-hand side of the window, click on the icon shaped like a *PCI* card with a plus sign to add a new network:

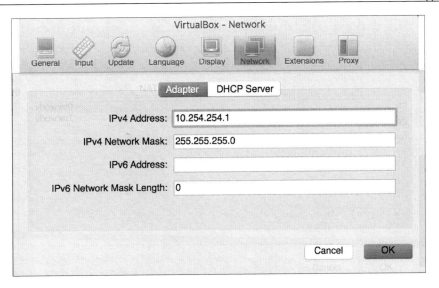

3. This network will be used as the management and OpenStack API network. Our client machine, in this case, the workstation running VirtualBox, needs an IP address from the network in order to communicate with the virtual machine hosting the OpenStack environment. Specify the address 10.254.254.1 and a netmask of 255.255.255.0. Be sure to disable DHCP in the **DHCP Server** section and click on the **OK** button to save the changes. Once the changes have been saved, the network will appear in the list:

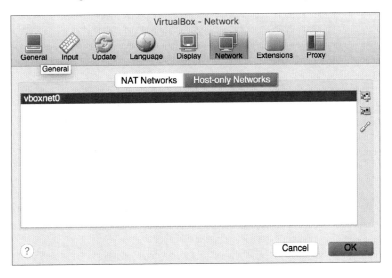

4. Click on the PCI card icon again to add an additional network that will be used to communicate with the external provider network created in this book:

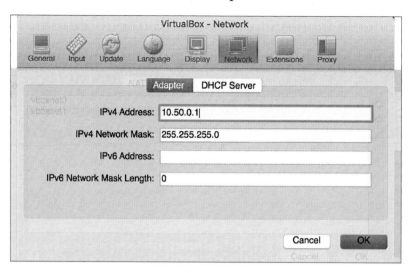

5. Click on **OK** to save the changes. Once they have been saved, both networks will be listed under **Host-only Networks**:

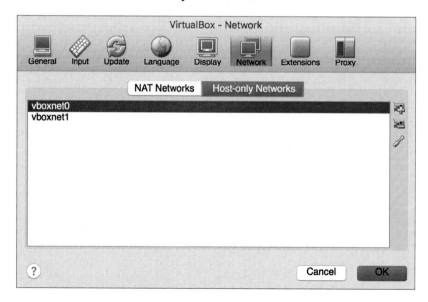

6. Click on **OK** to save the networks.

Creating a virtual machine

To create a virtual machine, follow these steps:

1. To create a virtual machine, click on the **New** icon in **Oracle VM VirtualBox Manager**:

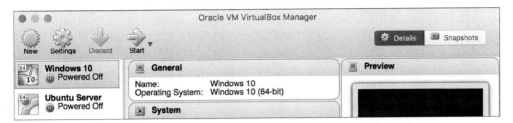

2. In the wizard, name the virtual machine, specify the operating system version (or something close to it), and click on **Continue**:

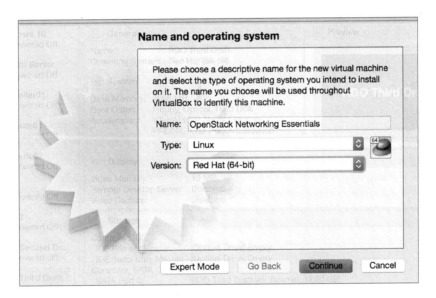

3. In the next window, specify the amount of memory to allocate to the virtual machine and click on **Continue**. A minimum of **4096 MB** of **RAM** is recommended.

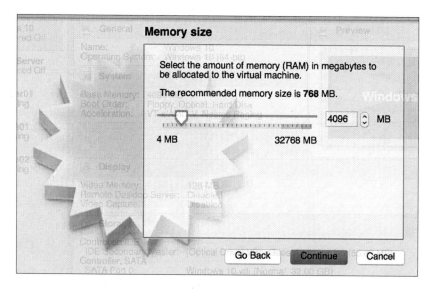

4. In the next window, click on **Continue** to create a virtual hard disk:

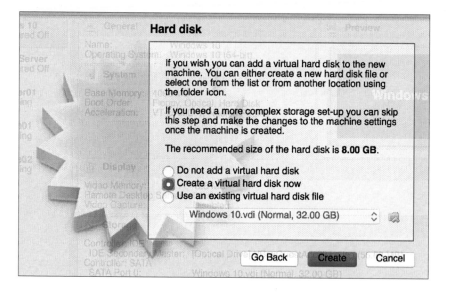

5. A hard disk wizard will appear that will allow you to specify the virtual hard disk type. Choose the default **VDI** image type and click on **Continue**:

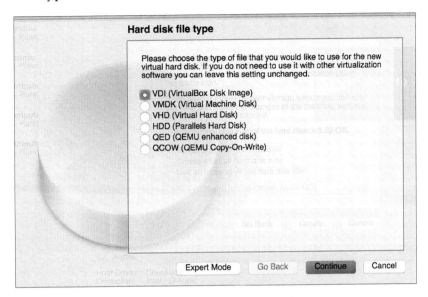

6. The next step of the wizard allows you to specify whether the disk should grow dynamically up to the maximum size as data is added or be fully allocated at creation. Choose your preference and click on **Continue**:

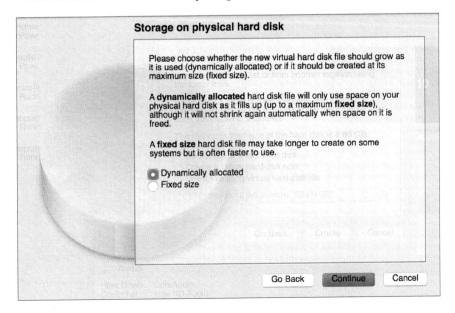

7. Lastly, provide a name for the virtual hard disk file and set the size of the disk to be created. For the examples in this book, a minimum of **12 GB** is recommended.

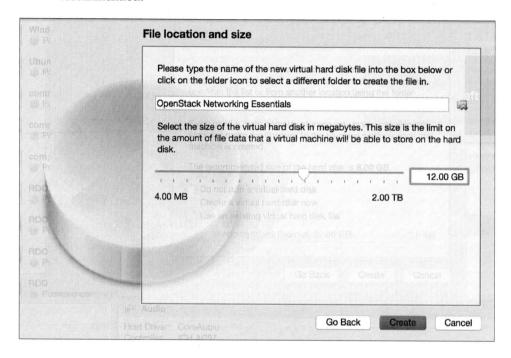

8. Click on the **Create** button to complete the creation of the virtual machine. The virtual machine will be listed in **Oracle VM VirtualBox Manager**:

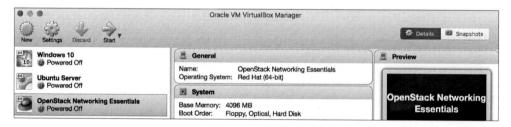

Configuring a virtual machine

Before the operating system is installed on the virtual machine, it is a good idea to configure the virtual network interfaces available to the machine. Follow these steps to configure the virtual machine:

1. From **Oracle VM VirtualBox Manager**, choose the virtual machine and click on the **Settings** icon. A window will appear that defaults to the **General** settings:

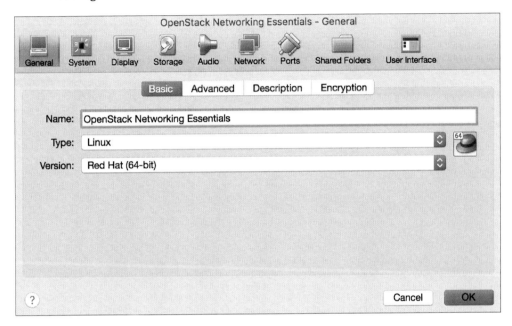

2. Click on the **Network** icon to modify the network interfaces presented to the virtual machine. The first adapter available, **Adapter 1**, should be enabled and attached to the vboxnet0 host-only network created earlier:

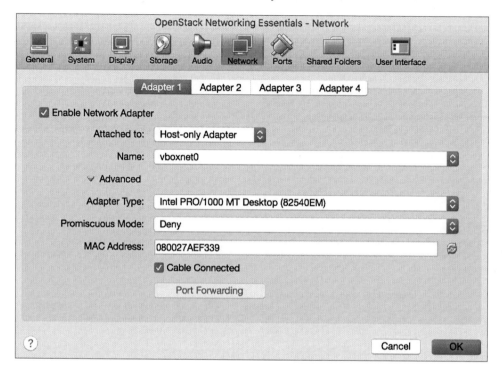

3. **Adapter 2** should be enabled and attached to the vboxnet1 host-only network created earlier. The **Promiscuous Mode** setting should be changed to **Allow All**:

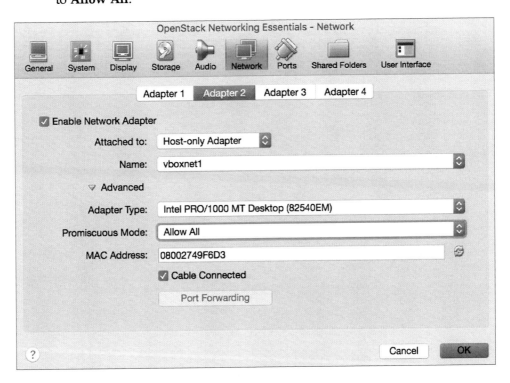

4. **Adapter 3** should be enabled and attached to the **NAT** network:

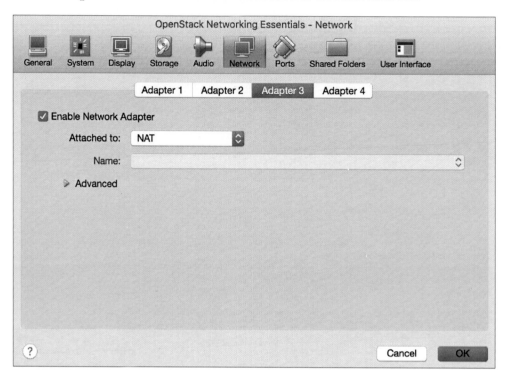

> By default, VirtualBox provides a **NAT** network that allows virtual machines to use the host machine for outbound network access. This network is required for the virtual OpenStack node to download the OpenStack software.

5. Click on the **OK** button to complete the network adapter configuration process and close the settings window.

Installing the CentOS operating system

Before an operating system can be installed, an ISO image must be downloaded from the Internet and attached to the virtual machine as a CD. The CentOS Server operating system can be downloaded from the following location:

`https://www.centos.org/download/.`

The minimal ISO is all that is required for a successful installation.

Attaching the ISO to the virtual machine

To attach ISO file to the virtual machine, follow these steps:

1. Once the ISO has been downloaded, choose the virtual machine in the **Oracle VM VirtualBox Manager** and click the **Settings** icon. Click on the **Storage** icon to manage storage options:

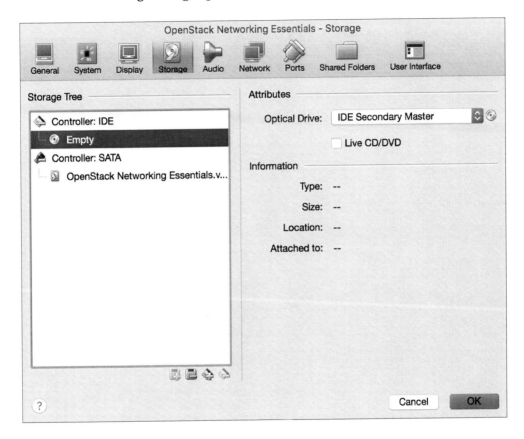

2. Click the first CD icon labeled **Empty** to modify the optical drive. Click the CD icon attach the downloaded ISO to the virtual machine. When prompted, click **Choose Virtual Optical Disk File** to find the ISO on the local machine:

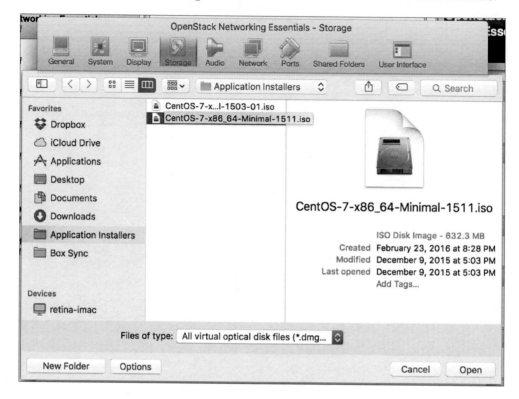

3. Select the ISO and click **Open** to attach the image. Once attached, the image will be listed under the **IDE** controller:

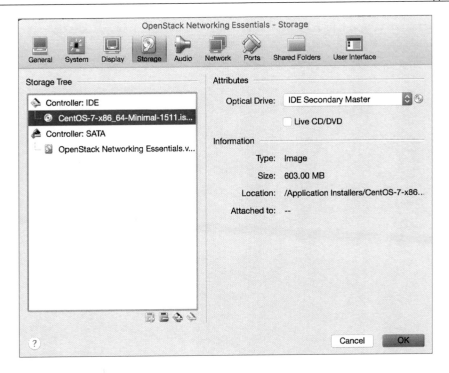

4. Click **OK** to close the settings window.

Starting the virtual machine

From the **Oracle VM VirtualBox Manager**, choose the virtual machine and click the **Start** icon:

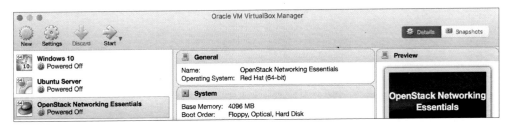

The virtual machine will boot off the CD image and present you with the installation screen:

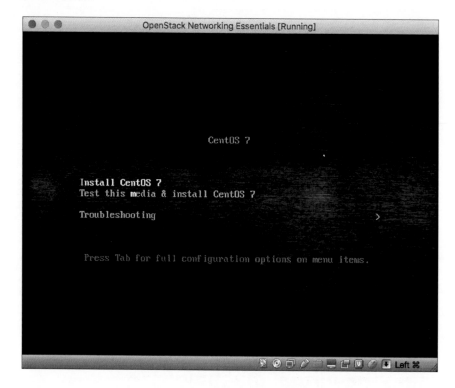

Choose **Install CentOS 7** from the menu. Installing the guest operating system is outside the scope of this book. However, there are plenty of guides available on the Internet, including the following from HowtoForge:

https://www.howtoforge.com/centos-7-server.

It is safe to ignore prompts to configure networking, as those tasks will be completed once the virtual machine is up and running.

Configuring virtual machine networking

Once the guest operating system has been installed, it is time to configure the networking within the virtual machine. This includes the setup of the management and NAT networks.

Accessing the virtual machine

Before networking has been configured, access to the virtual machine will be limited to the console. From the virtual machine console, enter the credentials specified during the installation process. A successful login should result in a screen similar to the following:

Use the `sudo` command to login as `root`:

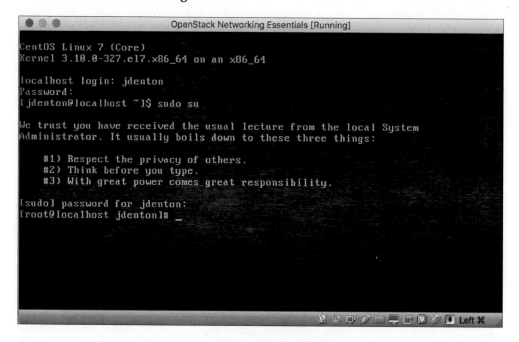

Configuring network interfaces

Using the `ip addr` command, verify that three network interfaces are attached to the virtual machine. The name of the network interfaces may vary from environment to environment:

```
● ● ●                OpenStack Networking Essentials [Running]
We trust you have received the usual lecture from the local System
Administrator. It usually boils down to these three things:

    #1) Respect the privacy of others.
    #2) Think before you type.
    #3) With great power comes great responsibility.

[sudo] password for jdenton:
[root@localhost jdenton]# ip a
1: lo: <LOOPBACK,UP,LOWER_UP> mtu 65536 qdisc noqueue state UNKNOWN
    link/loopback 00:00:00:00:00:00 brd 00:00:00:00:00:00
    inet 127.0.0.1/8 scope host lo
       valid_lft forever preferred_lft forever
    inet6 ::1/128 scope host
       valid_lft forever preferred_lft forever
2: enp0s3: <BROADCAST,MULTICAST,UP,LOWER_UP> mtu 1500 qdisc pfifo_fast state UP
qlen 1000
    link/ether 08:00:27:ae:f3:39 brd ff:ff:ff:ff:ff:ff
3: enp0s8: <BROADCAST,MULTICAST,UP,LOWER_UP> mtu 1500 qdisc pfifo_fast state UP
qlen 1000
    link/ether 08:00:27:49:f6:d3 brd ff:ff:ff:ff:ff:ff
4: enp0s9: <BROADCAST,MULTICAST,UP,LOWER_UP> mtu 1500 qdisc pfifo_fast state UP
qlen 1000
    link/ether 08:00:27:a6:4e:04 brd ff:ff:ff:ff:ff:ff
[root@localhost jdenton]# _
```

In this environment, the interfaces are named enp0s3, enp0s8, and enp0s9. Using a text editor, edit the network interface files found at /etc/sysconfig/network-scripts/ifcfg-* with the configuration provided in *Chapter 2, Installing OpenStack Using RDO*. Once configured, bring up the interfaces using the ifup command.

Accessing a virtual machine over SSH

Once networking has been configured on the virtual machine, it should be possible to access it over the management network via SSH from your client workstation. Within a terminal, SSH to the virtual machine using the username and password provided during installation:

```
retina-imac:~ jdenton$ ssh jdenton@10.254.254.100
The authenticity of host '10.254.254.100 (10.254.254.100)' can't be established.
ECDSA key fingerprint is SHA256:CvnFumO6vR46AgVX3xGoMa51CeMz5eWMKGk2HBZcnGg.
Are you sure you want to continue connecting (yes/no)? yes
Warning: Permanently added '10.254.254.100' (ECDSA) to the list of known hosts.
jdenton@10.254.254.100's password:
Last login: Sun Mar 20 13:09:10 2016
[jdenton@localhost ~]$
```

Use the `ping` command within the virtual machine to verify outbound connectivity to the Internet:

```
[jdenton@localhost ~]$ ping 8.8.8.8
PING 8.8.8.8 (8.8.8.8) 56(84) bytes of data.
64 bytes from 8.8.8.8: icmp_seq=1 ttl=63 time=32.9 ms
^C
--- 8.8.8.8 ping statistics ---
1 packets transmitted, 1 received, 0% packet loss, time 0ms
rtt min/avg/max/mdev = 32.990/32.990/32.990/0.000 ms
```

Once connectivity has been verified, you may proceed with the installation of OpenStack documented in *Chapter 2, Installing OpenStack Using RDO.*

Index

A

additional attributes 32
additional installation tasks
  about 23
  demo project and user, creating
  image, uploading to Glance 25, 26
  keystone_demo file, configuring 25
  security group rule, creating 23, 24
advanced networking features
  about 3
  firewalling 3
  load balancing 3
  virtual private networks 3
AMD-v technology 11

C

CentOS operating system
  installing 144
  ISO, attaching to virtual machine 145-147
  URL 144
  virtual machine, starting 147, 148
CentOS Server
  download link 11
Classless Inter-Domain Routing
    (CIDR) notation
  about 44, 123
  for controlling traffic 123
connectivity, through router
  about 72, 73
  inbound connectivity 74, 75
  outbound connectivity 74
core plugins 6

D

default security group 121, 122
DHCP agent 7
Distributed Virtual Router (DVR) 77
Dynamic Host Configuration Protocol
    (DHCP) 7

E

egress traffic 121

F

Firewall as a Service (FWaaS) 3, 117
flat network 59-61
floating IP 109
Forwarding Database (FDB) table 56

G

gateway interface 100
Generic Routing Encapsulation (GRE) 2
GRE network 65

H

Highly Available (HA) router 77
Horizon dashboard
  networks, creating within project 42-46
  network topology, viewing 46
  resources, managing as administrator 47-49
  resources, managing within project 42
  using 42

I

inbound connectivity 74, 75
initial network configuration
  about 12, 13
  example networks 13
  host, connecting to 16
  interface configuration 14-16
initial steps, OpenStack installation
  about 16
  hostname, setting 17
  NetworkManager, disabling 17
  Network Time Protocol (NTP), installing 17
  network utilities, installing 17
  permissions 16
  system upgrade 18
internal interface 100
Internet Protocol Security (IPSec) 3
IP Address Management (IPAM) system 6

K

Kernel-based Virtual Machine (KVM) 1

L

Link Aggregation Control Protocol
  (LACP) 2
LinuxBridge platform 55
LinuxBridge agent 56
LinuxBridge driver 56
Linux bridges
  using 56
Linux Containers (LXC) 1
Load Balancing as a Service (LBaaS) 3
Local Area Network (LAN) interface 100
local network 58, 59

M

mechanism drivers 7
metadata agent 7
Modular Layer 2 (ML2) plugin 2, 56

N

net-list command
  using 66-70

net-show command
  using 67-70
Network Address Translation (NAT) 133
network attributes
  about 30
  additional attributes 32
  provider attributes 31
Network Functions Virtualization
  (NFV) 130
network, implementing
  about 6
  DHCP agent 7
  metadata agent 7
  network plugin agent 8, 9
  Neutron agents 7
  plugins and drivers 6
Networking as a Service (NaaS) 1
networks 29, 30
network types 57
Neutron
  about 1, 27
  routing 71
Neutron agents 7
Neutron API
  about 27-29
  reference 29
Neutron client
  networks, creating 52
  networks, listing 51
  subnet, creating 53, 54
  using 50, 51
Neutron L3 agent 4
Neutron RBAC 31
Neutron router
  advanced networking 115, 116
  attaching, to external provider
    network 101, 102
  connectivity, testing 105-108
  connectivity, testing via floating IP 113, 114
  external provider networks 100
  floating IP, assigning 110-112
  instance, booting 103, 104
  multiple routers 114, 115
  SNAT behavior, observing 109
  using 98, 99
Neutron security groups
  characteristics 119

Neutron workflow
   about 37
   instance, booting 37
   instance, deleting 39
   logical model, implementing 37, 38
Nova Network 77

O

OpenStack
   security groups 118
   switching 55
   system requirements 11, 12
OpenStack architecture
   about 4, 5
   compute nodes 4
   controller nodes 4
   network nodes 4
   storage nodes 4
OpenStack documentation
   reference 50
OpenStack Networking
   about 1
   advanced networking features 3
   features 1, 2
   routing 2
   switching 2
OpenStack SDK
   reference 41
Open vSwitch
   about 55
   flow mode 56
   normal mode 56
   using 56
outbound connectivity 74
ovs-vsctl show command
   using 68

P

Packstack
   about 18
   used, for installing RDO
ports 34-36
port security
   about 129
   allowed address pairs 129
   disabling 130

provider attributes 31
provider bridge 57, 92
provider extension 31
provider networks
   creating 91, 92
   instance, accessing 94-97
   instance, booting 92-94
   using 89, 90

R

RDO
   answer file, configuring 18
   connectivity to dashboard, verifying 22, 23
   connectivity to OpenStack, verifying 21, 22
   downloading 18
   installing 20, 21
   installing, Packstack used 18
reference architecture
   about 6
   network, implementing 6
Remote SPAN (RSPAN) 2
Role Based Access Control
     (RBAC) functionality 31
router-gateway-set 101
router interface 100
router-interface-add 101
routers
   about 76
   Distributed Virtual Router (DVR) 77
   examining 86, 87
   Highly Available (HA) router 77
   standalone router 76
   types 76
routers, managing in dashboard
   about 78
   network topology, viewing 79-81
   routers, as administrator 82
   routers, creating within project 78, 79
routers, managing with Neutron client
   about 83
   interface, adding 84, 85
   router interfaces, listing 85
   routers, creating 83, 84
   routers, listing 83

routing
about 71
connectivity, through router 72, 73
network namespaces 71, 72
**RPM Distribution of OpenStack
(RDO) 11**

S

security groups
about 118
applying, to instances 127
applying, to instances and ports 124
caveats 128
CIDR, used for controlling traffic 123
creating 125
default security group 121, 122
managing 122
rules, managing 126
using 119-121
working with, in dashboard 125
service plugins 6
Software-Defined Networking (SDN) 56
**Source Network Address Translation
(SNAT) 71, 74**
standalone router 76
subnets 32, 33
switching
basics 55
flat networks 59-61
GRE networks 65
Linux bridges, using 56
local networks 58, 59
network types 57
Open vSwitch, using 56, 57
VLAN networks 61-63
VXLAN networks 63-65
Switch port Analyzer (SPAN) 2
system requirements 11

T

tenant networks 71
tunnel bridge 64
type drivers 7

V

VirtualBox networking
configuring 133
host-only networks, configuring 134-136
Virtual Extensible LAN (VXLAN) 2
**Virtual eXtensible Local Area Network
(VXLAN) 63**
Virtual Local Area Networks (VLANs) 29
virtual machine
accessing, over SSH 151
configuring 141-144
creating 137-140
virtual machine interfaces (VIFs) 34
virtual machine networking
configuring 149
network interfaces, configuring 150, 151
virtual machine, accessing 149
virtual network infrastructure
about 66
commands, using 66
**Virtual Private Network as a Service
(VPNaaS) 3**
**Virtual Router Redundancy Protocol
(VRRP) 129**
**Virtual Routing and Forwarding (VRF)
domains 71**
VLAN network 61-63
VT-x technology 11
VXLAN Network Identifier (VNI) 64
VXLAN networks 63-65
VXLAN Tunnel End Point (VTEP) 63

W

Wide Area Network (WAN) interface 100